T3-BLC-299

ARCHERY

AYNE C. McKINNEY

PHYSICAL
EDUCATION
ACTIVITIES
SERIES

ARCHERY

BROWN

PHYSICAL EDUCATION ACTIVITIES SERIES

Edited by:
AILEENE LOCKHART
University of Southern California
Los Angeles, California

Evaluation Materials Editor:
JANE A. MOTT
Smith College
Northampton, Massachusetts

BIOPHYSICAL VALUES OF MUSCULAR ACTIVITY, *E. C. Davis, Gene A. Logan, and Wayne C. McKinney*
ARCHERY, *Wayne C. McKinney*
BADMINTON, *Margaret Varner*
BOWLING, *Joan Martin*
CIRCUIT TRAINING, *Robert P. Sorani*
CONDITIONING FOR WOMEN, *Jane A. Mott*
FENCING, *Muriel Bower and Torao Mori*
FIELD HOCKEY, *Anne Delano*
GOLF, *Virginia L. Nance and E. C. Davis*
HANDBALL, *Michael Yessis*
ISOMETRIC EXERCISE, *William R. Pierson*
MEN'S BASKETBALL, *Glenn Wilkes*
MEN'S GYMNASTICS, *G. A. Broten*
MODERN DANCE, *Esther E. Pease*
PHYSICAL AND PHYSIOLOGICAL CONDITIONING FOR MEN, *Benjamin Ricci*
SKIN AND SCUBA DIVING, *Albert A. Tillman*
SOCCER, *Richard L. Nelson*
SOFTBALL, *Marian E. Kneer and Charles L. McCord*
SQUASH RACQUETS, *Margaret Varner and Norman Bramall*
SWIMMING, *Betty J. Vickers and William J. Vincent*
TENNIS, *Joan Johnson and Paul Xanthos*
TRACK AND FIELD, *Kenneth E. Foreman and Virginia L. Husted*
VOLLEYBALL, *Glen H. Egstrom and Frances Schaafsma*
WEIGHT TRAINING, *Philip J. Rasch*
WOMEN'S BASKETBALL, *Frances Schaafsma*
WOMEN'S GYMNASTICS, *A. Bruce Frederick*
WRESTLING, *Arnold Umbach and Warren R. Johnson*

PHYSICAL EDUCATION
ACTIVITIES SERIES

ARCHERY

WAYNE C. McKINNEY
Southwest Missouri State College

Illustrations by DIANE LOGAN

WM. C. BROWN COMPANY PUBLISHERS
DUBUQUE, IOWA

Library of Congress Catalog Card Number: 66–21272

Manufactured by WM. C. BROWN CO., INC., Dubuque, Iowa
Printed in U. S. A.

Preface

This book is designed for the beginning archery student at the college level. It introduces many facets of a sport which may be utilized avocationally throughout one's lifetime and gives a brief introduction to the historical role of archery. The text is intended to be more than a "how to shoot" book. It should give the serious student some insight regarding the importance of archery in the past and why it can be of value to the student in the future.

Guidelines are given for selection of archery tackle, and the latest concepts related to techniques of archery for beginners are discussed. Some potential values and ways of acquiring them are considered. The major emphases are placed on target archery and bow hunting.

Acknowledgment is made to Doug Kittredge, Hunting Editor of *Bow and Arrow* magazine. Our discussions of archery at the University of Southern California led indirectly to the writing of this book. Appreciation is also extended to Norman, Jack and Bob Wilson, three of the best bowyers in the United States, for their comments regarding the manuscript. The assistance of Linda and Bud Clay, who served as the archers for the illustrations, is appreciated. Dr. Gene A. Logan and Diane Logan are acknowledged for their assistance as art consultant and graphic artist respectively. Finally, I want to thank Dianna Porter for her help with the final manuscript.

The content and purpose of the book, together with possible errors, are, however, the sole responsibility of the author.

Self-evaluation questions are distributed throughout the text. These give the reader samples of the kinds of understanding and levels of skill that he should be acquiring as he progresses toward mastery of archery.

Wayne C. McKinney

Contents

1

Archery Tackle

The term "archery tackle" denotes the equipment an archer uses while shooting. There is an axiom which states that an athlete or sportsman will be as good or poor as his equipment. There is truth in that statement, especially in regard to archery. Tackle should be one of the *first* things considered by a person who is interested in learning this sport.

The beginner should give himself every opportunity to learn efficiently. This requires that archery tackle be *matched,* i.e., arrows, which are exactly alike in every detail, should be matched for use with a specific bow which, in turn, is suitable for a specific archer. Each archer differs in regard to strength, length of limbs, aesthetic likes and dislikes and so forth; consequently, tackle should be issued or purchased to suit individual needs and differences.

A beginner who is mismatched for his tackle will experience considerable frustration. It is possible with inferior tackle to do all fundamentals correctly and still have little success. With cheap or mismatched tackle each arrow shot could have a different flight pattern. As a result, arrow grouping would be erratic or nonexistent. Overcoming the human factors contributing to mistakes in accuracy is enough in and of itself to make archery a challenging sport for the beginner and expert alike. The archer should not use inefficient tackle which adds to the unique problems and challenges of learning to be accurate with the bow and arrow.

The beginning archer should start shooting with tackle issued to him by a qualified archery instructor. (To enhance learning, this tackle should be matched as nearly as possible for each archer.) Cost of tackle can be prohibitive for the student. He should try the sport for a period of time to determine whether or not he would like to pursue it further. If he becomes interested in archery as a lifetime sport, it is recommended that he purchase his own tackle from a professional archery shop. The usual sporting goods stores and department stores are poor places to purchase tackle *unless* their salesmen are cognizant of the technical aspects of archery tackle.

It is recommended that the archer who plans to use archery as an avocational activity purchase the following tackle: (1) twelve fiberglass or aluminum arrows with target points; (2) a recurve bow with center-shot design; (3) one leather finger tab; (4) one leather arm guard and (5) one arrow quiver. This matched tackle is enough to enable the archer to learn to shoot efficiently. The over-all cost depends upon the quality of the tackle. A principle to keep in mind is that *over-all cost should not be reduced by purchasing inexpensive arrows.* The arrow is the most important single item of tackle. A cheaper bow or a used bow could be purchased initially for the learning period. A more expensive bow could then be bought at a later date if desired.

THE ARROW

Arrows are manufactured from a wide variety of materials. As a result, prices range from the inexpensive, twenty-five cent arrow, to the expensive, two to three dollar arrow. Many different kinds of woods have been used by arrow makers in the past, but the most common on the market today are Port Orford cedar and birch. It must be noted, however, that wooden arrows are not used too frequently today by experienced and expert archers—more stable materials are available, namely fiberglass and aluminum.

Fiberglass arrows are recommended for archers who are learning the sport. These are manufactured with precision. During the past decade research has led to the development of a light and durable fiberglass material which is highly acceptable for quality arrow shafts. It is possible for arrow manufacturers to maintain quality control to the point that there are only microscopic deviations in regard to shaft thickness, shaft diameter and actual arrow weight. The same thing can not be said regarding wooden arrows, especially cheaper ones. In addition, the shaft of a fiberglass arrow will not warp like the shaft of a wooden arrow. The fiberglass arrow shaft always remains straight—this also is an advantage of the fiberglass arrow over the aluminum arrow shaft. The fiberglass, like the wooden arrow, will break if it strikes the target stand at an odd angle. The frequency with which this occurs is minimal but it happens less frequently with fiberglass than with wooden arrows. Fiberglass arrows can be smashed if stepped upon because the shafts are hollow. The novice

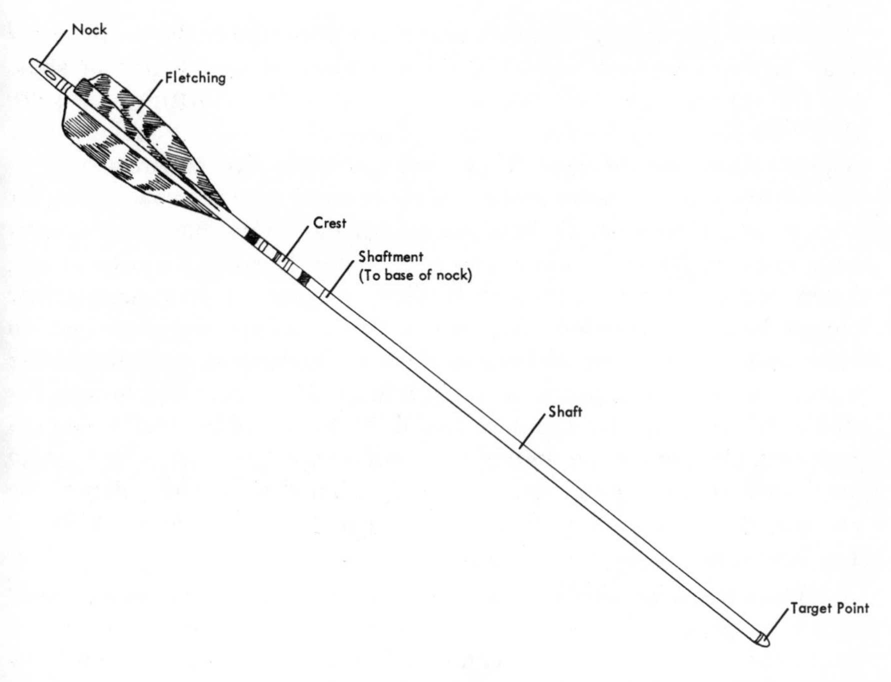

Figure 1—The Arrow

who uses a matched end of fiberglass arrows—six arrows with the same physical weight, degree of shaft stiffness (spine), length and fletching (feathers)—will shoot more accurately than the beginning archer who shoots unmatched or matched wooden arrows.

Aluminum arrows are the finest and most accurate on the market today. Aluminum alloys allow manufacturers to construct arrows that are nearly perfect. When shot by a machine during tests from fifty yards, it is not uncommon to see arrows grouped within a diameter of two inches. Aluminum arrows are, however, the most expensive arrows on the market. If the beginner wants to purchase an end of aluminum arrows, he should keep the following facts in mind: (1) he will miss the target completely on occasions and lose arrows—amounting to dollars—in the grass and (2) aluminum arrow shafts, unlike fiberglass arrows, will bend when they strike the target stand or other hard objects instead of the target mat. There are techniques and procedures which can be used to straighten a bent aluminum shaft, however. If the beginner accepts these facts prior to purchase, aluminum arrows are recommended for him as well as for the expert archer.

Spine—Spine simply refers to the degree of flexibility within the shaft of an arrow. There are instruments which measure the degree of spine with minute precision. The degree of spine is the basic thing to consider when obtaining arrows and should be compatible with the archer's bow weight. One reason for this is a phenomenon known as the *Archer's Paradox*. Contrary to what the archer thinks he sees as the arrow leaves his bow, an arrow does not fly straight toward the target immediately upon being released. By means of cinematographical analysis, it has been clearly shown that the arrow shaft actually bends around the bow immediately after it has been released. The reader can readily understand that an arrow shaft which is too stiff or too flexible could cause problems during this phase of its flight pattern. An arrow of sufficient spine, *which has been released properly,* tends to stabilize itself rapidly and follows a straight flight pattern on its path toward the target. The fact that an arrow first deviates to the left for a right-handed archer as it leaves the bow but stabilizes itself in flight to travel directly to its intended target is known as the *Archer's Paradox.*

What are some of the consequences of having improperly spined arrows for a bow? (It must be kept in mind that several factors other than spine are also involved with accurate arrow flight. These will be discussed later.) Improper spine can cause the following arrow flight patterns: (1) an arrow naturally starts its flight by deviating a few degrees to the left for a right-handed archer. If the spine is *too stiff,* the shaft of the arrow or the fletching will actually brush the bow. This causes a reduction in arrow speed. In addition, a flight pattern change occurs in the opposite direction. The archer's shot will be low on the target—or in the grass—and to the right of the intended target and (2) if the spine is *too weak or too flexible,* the arrow may never stabilize into its intended flight pattern but will fly consistently to the left. Improperly spined arrows are a definite causative factor for erratic arrow grouping.

What should be considered when selecting the proper spine for arrows? First, the bow weight, i.e., the pounds of pull exerted on the bow string by the archer for his specific arrow length, is very important. Second, the arrow length and arrow weight to the grain must be known accurately. Third, the type and weight of the arrow point is also a basic consideration. Tackle manufacturers have designed sophisticated devices to measure spine, and charts with norms and standards are available to help the archer match his arrows to the bow of his choice. A heavier arrow with a heavier arrow point generally will require stiffer spine. An archer should not be satisfied with generalities, however, when selecting arrows for *his* bow! Correct spine can mean the difference between a score of nine and a complete miss in a target archery tournament or between a deer and a lost arrow during bow hunting season.

Fletching—The feathers of an arrow are known collectively as fletching. The fletching of an arrow is as important to it as the tail assembly is to an airplane. The function of the two analogous parts is essentially the same, i.e., they both serve to stabilize the flight patterns of the airborne objects. The fletching stabilizes the arrow by channeling, as much as possible, the wind currents which the arrow encounters during flight. This stabilization assists the arrow in maintaining rotation around its horizontal axis while in flight.

Fletching is available in the form of feathers from turkeys or imitation feathers of plastic and rubber. The actual number of feathers or vanes on an arrow ranges from three to eight. Most archers prefer three or four vane fletching. Three vane, turkey feather fletching is good for use in target archery. Feathers three and one-half inches in length are recommended for beginners. It is recommended that fletching be lengthened to five inches for use in bow hunting situations. The main reason for the added length is the considerable difference in weight between the target point and the broadhead point used in bow hunting. The larger fletching is needed to add flight stability for the heavier hunting arrow.

Fletching is usually colored in a distinct and traditional manner. On an arrow which has three vanes, two vanes will be drab in color and one vane will be rather flamboyant. The two drab vanes are called "hen feathers" and the brightly colored vane is known as the "cock feather." This terminology has an ornithological origin, i.e., male birds are usually more spectacular in color than female birds.

The cock feather traditionally is placed so it points outward from the bow when the arrow is nocked or placed in the bow string. It is recommended that experienced archers try shooting with the cock feather downward or toward the bow periodically. Flight patterns shot both ways should be evaluated for a period of time. The best technique of fletching placement should be adopted permanently after a satisfactory evaluation period. The archer may actually find that his arrows will have a tendency to fly better when the arrow is nocked with the hen feathers outward. Arrows are designed, however, to be shot with the cock feather upward. An experienced archer may experiment with his arrow nock by rotating it.

Arrow Length—The actual length of the arrow varies for each individual, being determined by arm length. This can be done by either of the following methods:

1. Determine the anchor point, the placement of the archer's bowstring hand on the face with the bow at full draw, and measure with a tape measure to the back of the bow. This gives the arrow length.
2. Measure the total arm span in inches from the distal end of the left, middle finger to the distal end of the right, middle finger. Thirty-eight per cent of that figure gives the arrow length in inches.

The beginner should allow an additional inch for his arrows. He will find that anchor point adjustments must be made, and it is better to have arrows too long than too short. Bow hunters should also allow an additional inch for the larger arrow point. Arm spread is usually very close to height in inches, but height should never be used as a substitute for actual arm span measurement.

Arrow Points—Arrow points or arrow piles are manufactured in a wide variety of assortments and sizes. There are many special points for target archery, field archery, bow hunting and bow fishing. The beginning archer should start with light parallel points for target archery (Figure 1). After he masters the fundamentals of target archery, new arrow points may be purchased for field archery, bow hunting or bow fishing.

Figure 2 shows a three-bladed broadhead arrow point which is commonly used by bow hunters. This is a very heavy point, 125 grains. This design has been popular with bow hunters; however, blades with two and four cutting edges are increasing in popularity. The two-bladed hunting point may be the most efficient of the current designs on the market. The number of cutting surfaces is actually a matter of preference. The number is not the most important consideration, rather it is the degree of sharpness. *A bow hunting arrow point should be razor sharp!* In fact, some broadheads are designed specifically for injector razor blades. A dull hunting arrow is almost useless to the bow hunter unless he is hunting for very small game.

Figure 3 shows a diagram of a bird hunting arrow point which consists of steel wire loops. These four loops measure a total of six inches in diameter. The bow hunter must attempt to strike some portion of the game bird with the wire loops while it is in flight! This puts sport back into bird hunting. These large arrow points are used with flu-flu fletching, large feathers which are spiraled around the shaft to create air resistance. This diminishes the total distance the arrow will travel. This, of course, has the distinct advantage of reducing the number of lost arrows during the duration of the bird hunting season.

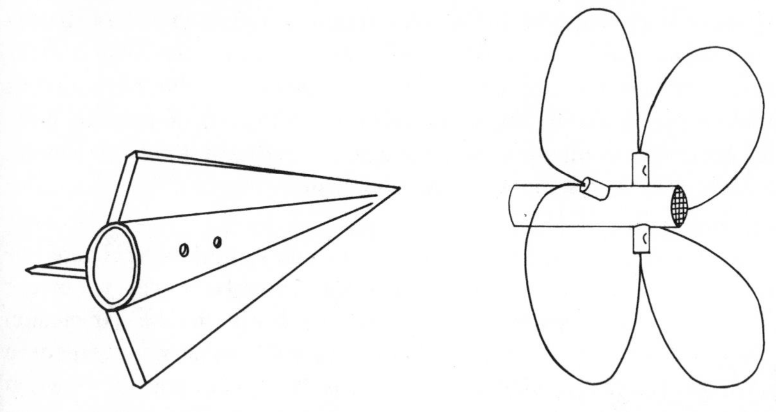

Figure 2—Broadhead Hunting Point *Figure 3—Bird Hunting Point*

Figure 4 shows a two barbed bow fishing point. Like broadheads for bow hunting, there are many different styles on the market. The "best" bow fishing point style is usually a matter of individual preference of the bow fisherman. These points are very heavy. Some weigh as much as 400 grains.

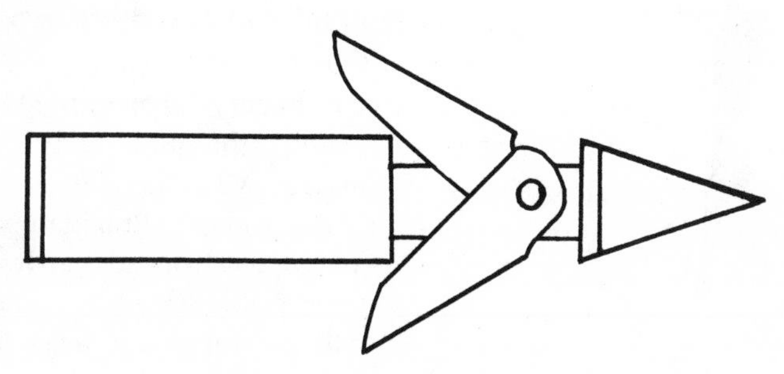

Figure 4—Bow Fishing Point

THE BOW

The bow has fascinated men for centuries. Men have used it for killing animals, killing enemies, making music, drilling holes in the ground and for sport.

Man has built bows in all shapes and sizes. As examples, the Asian uses a seven foot bow with straight, uneven limbs; the African uses a three foot bow with straight, even limbs; the Englishmen used a five foot long bow with straight limbs of varying lengths. Warriors at the Temple of Aigina used bows with duo-flexed limbs; the Apache Indians of America used a crude and very short bow; modern archery champions use bows like or similar to the bow shown in Figure 5, a recurve bow. Finally at least one contemporary archer who is almost a living legend, Howard Hill, uses the same type of bow which was employed by the English at the Battle of Hastings.

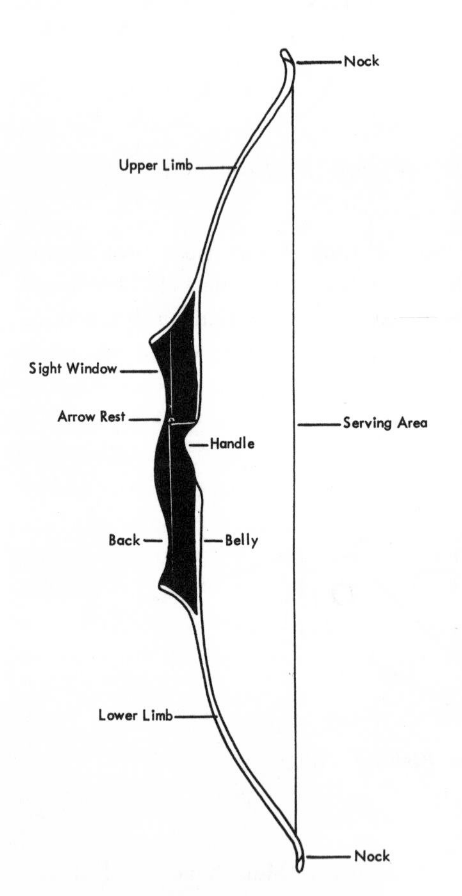

Figure 5–Recurve Bow

Which type is best? There are many arguments; however, current evidence leads to the conclusion that a well constructed recurve bow is the most efficient bow on the market. As an example, the Black Widow 101, manufactured by Norman, Jack and Bob Wilson of Springfield, Missouri, is an excellent and highly efficient multi-purpose recurve bow (Figure 5). There are many other highly efficient recurve bows for the archer to evaluate. These good bows range in price from forty to two hundred dollars each.

Recurve bows built of laminated fiberglass and hard rock maple with handle sections of black walnut, Brazilian rosewood and other tropical hardwoods are very stable shooting bows. They will last for many years if treated properly.

The weight of the bow is very important. Due to the force potential of a recurve bow, an all-purpose bow weight of thirty-five to forty-five pounds is recommended for experienced men archers and twenty to thirty pounds for experienced women archers. These bow weights are functional for target archery, bow hunting and field archery.

Bow weights are determined according to the number of pounds required to pull the bowstring back to full draw for a given arrow length. Most bows are marked for bow weight at a twenty-eight inch draw. This can usually be seen on the bow's handle section, lower limb. As the draw diminishes in length, the bow weight also diminishes in pounds, i.e., a person using a twenty-six inch arrow would not be pulling the same amount of bow weight as a person who uses a twenty-eight inch arrow.

A beginner should use a lighter bow than an experienced archer. It is easier to learn with the lighter weight bow. The novice should use a bow weight somewhere between twenty and twenty-five pounds. As skill increases, bow weight may be increased proportionately. Some women, although highly skilled, prefer to use lightweight bows.

Many archers, particularly some bow hunters and many adolescent boys, like to think that they need a heavy bow weight. Let us consider what actually happens when the potential kinetic energy of a bow is doubled. What are the differences in terms of arrow velocity between a forty-five pound and a ninety-pound bow? Will arrow velocity be doubled? Tripled? Taking variable arrow weights into consideration, it has been established that a ninety-pound bow adds an increase of only nineteen to twenty-five per cent to the velocity of the arrow over a bow weight of forty-five pounds. When an archer considers such factors as ease of handling, shooting over a prolonged period of time and accuracy difficulties, is a heavy bow really worth the effort? Most modern archers would answer in the negative.

Let us consider some of the basic differences between the recurve bow and the older, long bow. First, it should be noted that all recurve bows do not have recurve actions. In order to work efficiently, the bow string of the recurve bow must actually touch the belly of the bow for two to three inches adjacent to both nocks. If the bow is not designed in this manner, it will respond essentially the same as the long bow. When the bowstring touches the recurved bow tips as described, this tends to increase the leverage potential. A recurve bow of forty-five pounds will project an arrow at a rate of speed twenty per cent greater than a long bow of comparable weight. A modern recurve bow tends to draw more smoothly than a long bow because there is very little increase of weight during the last few inches of draw to the archer's anchor point—finger placement of the bowstring hand on the chin. (The phenomenon of ever-increasing weight as one draws the bowstring hand toward the face is known as "stacking.") Due to the increased arrow velocity which is derived through increased leverage, the recurve bow tends to project the

What criterion must be met for a recurve bow to be judged more efficient than a long bow?

Evaluation Questions

arrow on a flatter trajectory than a long bow thus adding scoring effectiveness. Finally, the semicircular configuration of the long bow, which is seen as it is being drawn, tends to cause an uneven distribution of stress in the limbs. This factor also tends to detract from the over-all efficiency and longevity of the long bow. The same phenomenon is not seen in the good recurve bow. Except in the hands of expert archers who have been using the long bow throughout their lifetimes, *the long bow should be retired to the museum!*

A good bow has a section cut away at the mid-line of its upper limb immediately above the arrow rest. This is called centershot design and the cutaway area is the sight window. This feature minimizes the components of the Archer's Paradox because the arrow is able to move past the bow in a path very close to the bowstring alignment with the belly of the bow. Another very important feature of a bow with centershot design is the practical aspect of letting the archer see his intended target! This is another argument in favor of the recurve bow.

Bow Length—Bows are manufactured in lengths ranging from fifty-two to seventy-two inches. The popularity of the shorter bows seems to be on the decline. Many bow hunters purchased the shorter bows specifically for hunting purposes. (This will be discussed in Chapter 4.) Many archers have now traded short bows in on bows ranging in length from sixty-four to seventy inches. Bows of these lengths can be used effectively for hunting *and* target archery.

Many target archers use bows ranging from sixty-eight to seventy inches in length. The added length minimizes the pressure exerted by the bowstring fingers on the arrow nock at the time of release. In addition, the longer bows actually weigh more. This factor helps to give the tournament archer a steadier bow hand while he is shooting.

The length of the draw is also a basic consideration for an individual who is selecting a target bow:

1. Twenty-seven inch draw—sixty-two inch bow is recommended.
2. Twenty-eight inch draw—sixty-four inch bow is recommended.
3. Twenty-nine inch draw—sixty-six inch bow is recommended.
4. Thirty and thirty-one inch draws—sixty-eight inch bow is recommended.

Hunting bows are designed to take draws up to thirty-one inches.

Bow Sights—Figure 6 shows a standard bow sight. Bow sights can be mounted on the back or the belly of the bow immediately above the arrow rest. (The use of the bow sight is described in Chapter 2.) There

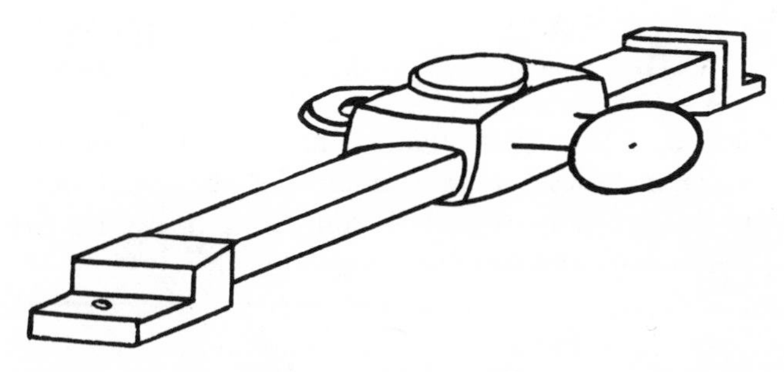

Figure 6—Bow Sight

are many commercial bow sights which range from inexpensive models such as the one shown in Figure 6 to very expensive models, which are manufactured by one major optical company.

The beginner is encouraged to use a bow sight after he becomes acquainted with the basic fundamentals. Two inexpensive methods for constructing a bow sight are described.

1. Materials needed are (1) one tongue blade, (2) one bobby pin and (3) adhesive tape. The tongue blade is mounted on the back of the bow just above the arrow rest. The bobby pin is fastened or clamped over the tongue blade so it will extend into the sight window and slide up and down the tongue blade. The tip of the bobby pin is used for target alignments.

2. Materials needed are (1) small strip of cork, one-fourth inch in thickness, and cut to fit the width of the back of the bow—total length approximately six inches; (2) one pin with a large-beaded, black head and (3) glue or adhesive tape. The cork strip is attached to the back of the bow above the arrow rest. The beaded pin is inserted into the cork so the pin head protrudes into the sight window area. The pin can be moved up and down as needed.

These two bow sights cost pennies, but they are just as efficient as more elaborate sights. The principles utilized in bow sights are the same regardless of their cost.

Some beginning archers may have point-of-aim markers and other point-of-aim materials to use as sighting devices. These materials should be taken to the museum along with the long bows! The point-of-aim method for sighting or aiming is no longer used. Bow sights are being used extensively in target archery tournaments where they are allowed. Furthermore, bow sights are being used more extensively by bow hunters.

ACCESSORIES

The archer must have protection for his bow arm and his bowstring fingers. Two common leather accessories, the finger tab and the arm guard, are shown in Figures 7 and 8. Both come in several sizes, shapes and styles. They are relatively inexpensive.

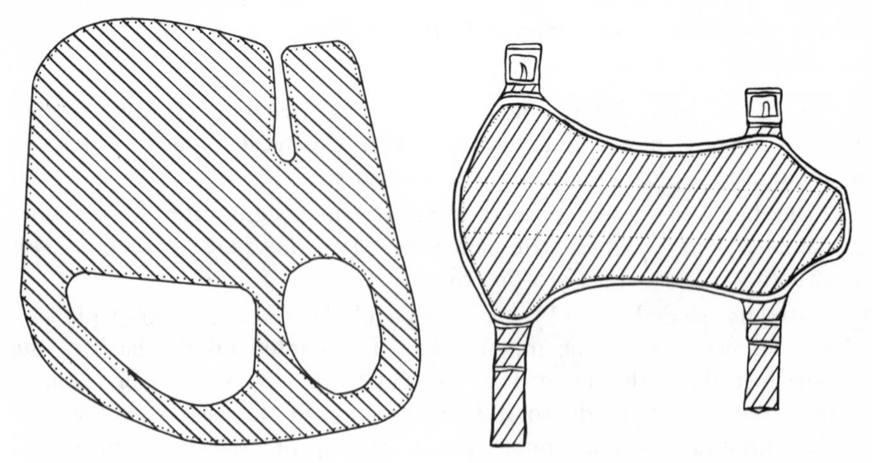

Figure 7—Finger Tab

Figure 8—Arm Guard

The finger tab is rather awkward to use at first, but it is absolutely essential for prolonged shooting, for otherwise the fingers will become very inflamed and irritated. Tender skin may become blistered because of the friction created when the bowstring rolls over the finger tips when the arrow is released.

The finger tab is placed on the bowstring hand. Most tabs have a rough and a smooth surface. The tab is placed over the fingers so the rough side is skyward. The index finger is placed through the smallest hole and the second and third fingers are placed through the largest hole. The tab is then bent so the smooth surface makes contact with the bowstring as the arrow is nocked and drawn. Many archers prefer shooting gloves instead of finger tabs. There are many styles available. (Figure 14.)

The arm guard is placed on the bow arm between the elbow and wrist, but nearer the wrist. This is an area which is "slapped" periodically by the bowstring. Shooting without an arm guard can result in serious contusions. Furthermore, following one severe blow by the bowstring on an unprotected arm, an archer has a tendency to flinch—flex the elbow and/or flex the wrist—when he releases the arrow. These are bad habits which the protection afforded by the arm guard tends to eliminate.

An arrow quiver is another accessory which the archer must obtain. This is a device designed to carry arrows. There are shoulder quivers, hip quivers, ground quivers and bow quivers. They come in all sizes, shapes and materials. Most beginners rely upon the inexpensive, metal ground quiver. The most commonly used quiver, however, is the hip quiver. The bow quiver seems to be gaining in popularity among bow hunters, because it attaches to the bow and eliminates carrying an extra object. Furthermore, the bow quiver makes the arrows more accessible to the bow hunter for that possible second shot at his game animal.

CARE OF ARCHERY TACKLE

The Bow—The following care and treatment of a bow will add to its longevity and effectiveness.

1. Always unstring your bow after use.
2. Place the bow in a flannel bowcase for storage purposes.
3. Lay the bow in a flat place or hang it vertically.
4. Wax the bow as needed with furniture wax.
5. Use beeswax on the bowstring to minimize fraying.
6. Do not drop the bow or leave it lying on the ground.

7. Draw the bow several times to your draw length prior to actually shooting an arrow.

Arrows—The following care and treatment of arrows will add to their longevity and effectiveness.

1. Store arrows in an arrow case.
2. Wipe arrows clean after shooting.
3. Apply a light coat of wax periodically.
4. Check fletching periodically—fletching can be replaced at a low cost.
5. Check arrow points for dullness or damage—points can be replaced.
6. Do not carry your arrows in your fist; this damages the fletching.

2

Fundamentals of Target Archery

Practicing archery fundamentals in front of a target is an absolute essential for future success in tournaments as well as in bow hunting and other archery events. As in any other sport, basic techniques of archery have been modified by individuals and champions. People have their theories, preferences and styles which have been developed through years of competition and practice. However, the basic fundamentals of archery, which are accepted as good form for beginners, are discussed in this chapter. Variations of basic form and style are discussed on occasions. The beginner may want to try these variations but this should be done only *after* he becomes familiar with his tackle and has practiced basic shooting techniques thoroughly.

THE ARCHER AND SAFETY

The archer should keep the following concept in mind when he has his tackle in hand: *archery is not a dangerous sport, but the bow and arrow does have lethal potential.* As a consequence, respect should be shown for one's tackle and for human beings both on the archery range and within shooting distance.

Safety rules vary slightly from range to range. All rules, however, incorporate good common sense and the concept of always being aware of the whereabouts of your fellow archers. When an arrow is placed in a bow it should be pointed only in the direction of the intended target, and the archer should know beyond all doubt that no other human being is within arrow distance of his intended target. This is easier to ascertain on target archery ranges than on field archery ranges or in bow hunting situations. Archery instructors usually have standard procedures which they design for practices at their ranges. These safety rules are usually posted or announced. When followed in detail, archery is one of the safest of sports.

The archer should go to the range in comfortable clothing. Loose fitting sweaters, shirts or blouses, however, are counterindicated because they can become entangled with the bowstring after it has been released. A bowstring, for example, which catches a button on a blouse or shirt may rip the garment causing unnecessary embarrassment and loss of personal property. Jewelry, such as watches, bracelets and pins, should not be worn on the archery range. These may be lost or damaged.

BRACING

Bracing the bow simply means to attach the bowstring to the bow in preparation for shooting. A bow should never be stored while it is braced for continuous tension on the bow limbs lessens the effectiveness and longevity of the bow.

There are two standard forms for bracing a bow manually: (1) the push-pull method and (2) the step-through method. The method used by the archer depends upon the weight of the bow and the strength of the individual. There are mechanical bow bracing devices available. These are recommended for use in colleges.

For most lightweight bows and for archers of average strength, the push-pull method of bracing is adequate. The following bracing steps are for right-handed archers:

1. Place the lower limb of the bow against the instep of the right foot; be certain that the bowstring is nocked on the lower limb of the bow.
2. Grasp the bow handle with the right hand.
3. Grasp the loop of the bowstring with the thumb and index finger of the left hand and slide it up the upper limb toward the nock of the bow.
4. PULL with the right hand and PUSH down on the upper limb with the left hand while sliding the bowstring loop upward and into the bow neck. *For safety purposes, keep the face out of alignment with the upper limb.*
5. Check to see that both bowstring loops are properly inserted in the bow nocks as a final safety precaution.

The *step-through method* of bracing should be used on the heavier recurve bows and by weaker individuals. The following bracing steps are for right-handed archers:

1. Assume an upright stance with the feet shoulder width apart.
2. *Step-through* or between the bowstring and the belly of the bow with the right leg.
3. See that the recurve of the lower limb encircles the left ankle.
4. Taking advantage of the leverage which this bow position allows, grasp the upper limb and bend it forward and downward with the right hand.
5. Move the bowstring loop upward, placing it in the nock with the left hand as the upper limb is being bent.
6. Check both nocks to see that the bowstring is properly inserted in them prior to shooting.

One word of caution should be noted regarding the step-through method of bracing. If the bow should slip during this procedure, cuffs of slacks, nylon hose and the like can be ripped. Steady pressure should be exerted and proper placement of the recurve around the left ankle should be checked to prevent the occurrence of that problem.

The actual distance from the bowstring to the handle of the bow is very important. This is known as the *fistmele* distance, because in ancient times this distance was measured by using the fist and an extended thumb. This is still a good technique to use as an approximate measure; however, most bow manufacturers indicate exactly what the fistmele distance should be for their bows. The archer should measure this distance accurately after the bow has been braced. A bowstring too close or too far from the belly of the bow will adversely affect arrow velocity and arrow flight. The bowstring can be twisted in order to make fistmele distance adjustments.

STANCE

The right-handed archer stands with his left side toward the intended target (Figure 9). The feet should be shoulder width apart. It is recommended that the body weight be distributed evenly on both feet initially. If a shooting line is marked on the range, it should be straddled by the archer. Placement of the feet is very important. The archer should stand with his feet in a position so an imaginary line can be drawn through his insteps to the center of the gold on the target face. The left foot should then be moved backwards approximately six inches. This is called the *open stance,* and it is recommended for those learning to shoot the bow and arrow.

The archer's stance must be consistent. The exact placement of the feet on the shooting line should be marked. This procedure enables the archer to return to exactly the same spot after he has retrieved his arrows from the target. Stance deviations of even a few inches can cause sighting and aiming problems. This, of course, causes subsequent accuracy problems. *Consistency* is a key word in archery.

Some expert archers distribute their body weight so the leg away from the target bears most of the weight. Many excellent archers also place the foot nearer the target so the instep is aligned with the toes of the foot farther from the target. These stance adjustments are usually made after several years of shooting. Many times these minor adjustments are made to compensate for minute errors elsewhere in shooting form, or they are made to adapt the stance to a particular anatomical peculiarity. In any event, the beginning archer should rely upon his instructor to make his stance adjustments.

If a ground quiver is used, Figure 9, it should be placed directly on the shooting line in front of the archer so arrows can be taken from it without any movement of the feet.

Figure 10 shows the very simple *one-quarter turn* of the archer's head toward his intended target. This very simple act tends to be so complex that it causes many beginners difficulty. If the following prin-

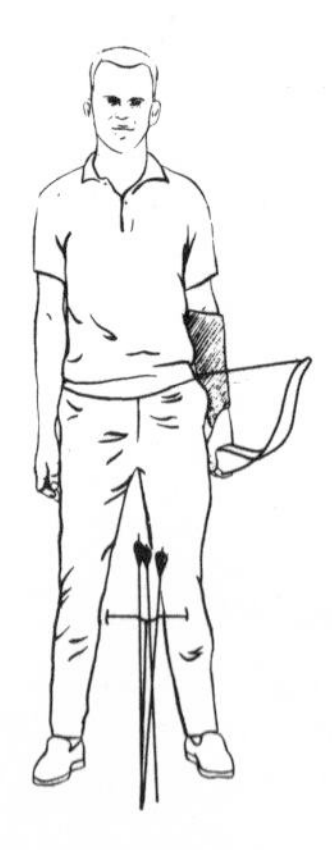

Figure 9—Basic Stance

Figure 10—Stance-Head Position

ciple is observed, no problem should be encountered: *the bowstring should be drawn to the head instead of moving the head to the bowstring*. Some beginners tend to move the head forward or flex the neck to meet the bowstring as it is being drawn. Such practices tend only to complicate matters. The head must remain in the position shown in Figure 10 at all times during the process of shooting. A slight movement of the chin may be necessary to allow for better placement of the bowstring hand on the face, but this adjustment should be done by the instructor if and when necessary.

NOCKING

Nocking the arrow, placement of the arrow in shooting position on the bowstring, is an important step in preparation for shooting. In target archery, this is done when all archers have assumed their stances on the shooting line. The archer holds the bow horizontal to the ground next to his hip nearest the target. The arrow shaft is laid on the bow and the arrow nock is placed on the bowstring at the serving, the middle portion of the bowstring which is wrapped with protective thread. Some bowstrings are equipped with rubber or plastic nocking devices.

The beginner should start by nocking his arrow so a ninety degree angle is formed between the arrow and bowstring. This is the traditional nocking angle (Figure 11). If consistent vertical fluctuations are noted in the flight pattern of the arrows after several weeks of practice, the archer should try moving his nocking point upward one-eighth to one-quarter of an inch (Figure 12). This adjustment may help correct the arrow flight problems.

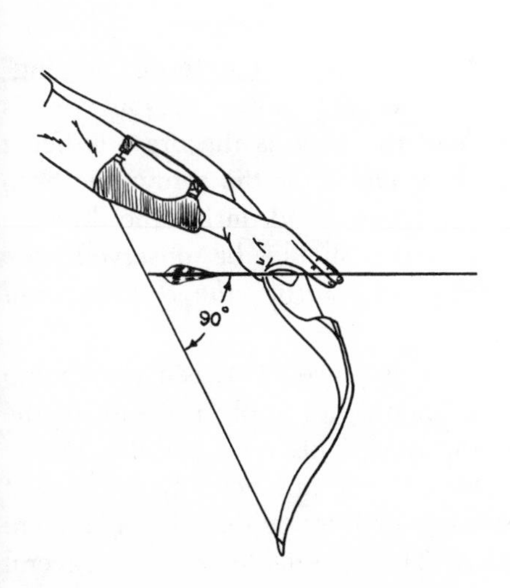

Figure 11—Traditional Nocking Angle

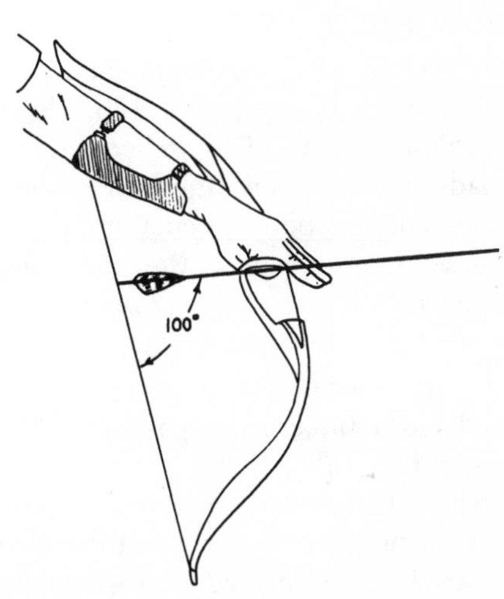

Figure 12—Nocking Angle Adjustment

What is the term for this stance?

Evaluation Questions
STANCE

The beginner should start by nocking with the cock feather projecting outward or away from the bow handle. This practice should be followed until the archer becomes familiar with his tackle and shooting procedures. It is recommended that some shooting be done with the hen feathers placed in the nocking position so they project outward. Flight patterns should be compared while shooting with the fletching in both nocking positions. The archer should use the nocking procedure which gives him the best results in terms of arrow stability in flight.

BOW HOLD

When used in conjunction with the bow hand the term "holding" is really a misnomer. It is misleading, especially to the person who is learning archery. The archer *does not hold* the bow as the draw is being made. He does hold the bow while nocking and after the arrow has been released. The bow is actually *pushed* by the bow hand during the drawing phase. Consequently, the following principle should be observed: *the bow should never be gripped or held tightly during the drawing and aiming phases of shooting.*

As can be seen in Figure 13, the bow is placed between the thumb and index finger. The palm of the hand should not apply pressure to the bow. The index finger wraps around the bow. This adds stability. Some archers like to have the thumb and index finger tips actually touch, but this is not necessary. The three remaining fingers on the bow hand are relaxed in an extended position. Why? This lessens fatigue in several muscles within the hand and forearm. Muscle tremor is reduced and this enhances accuracy.

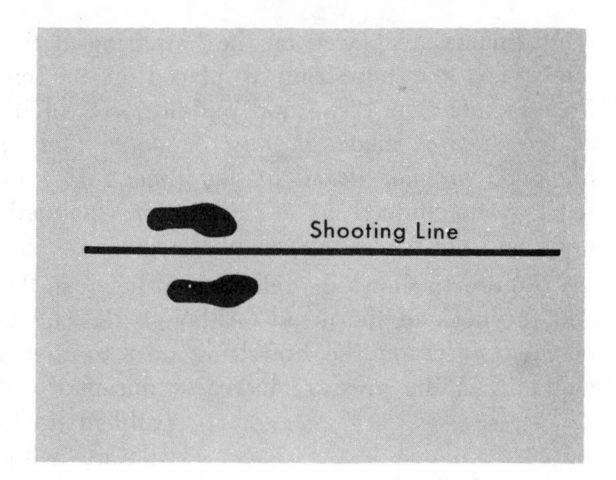

Diagram A:
STANCE

DRAWING

Drawing is the act of pulling the bowstring to the anchor point on the face. It is analogous to cocking a pistol prior to firing a bullet. One major difference is that there are many more opportunities for human error while drawing a bowstring than while cocking a pistol. Drawing may start as soon as the arrow is nocked properly. The breath is held from the time the anchor is established until the time of the release. The archer exhales at the time of release. The time amounts to approximately two to three seconds for most archers.

Figure 14 shows the commonly used three finger bowstring grip. The little finger and thumb do not touch the bowstring. The remaining

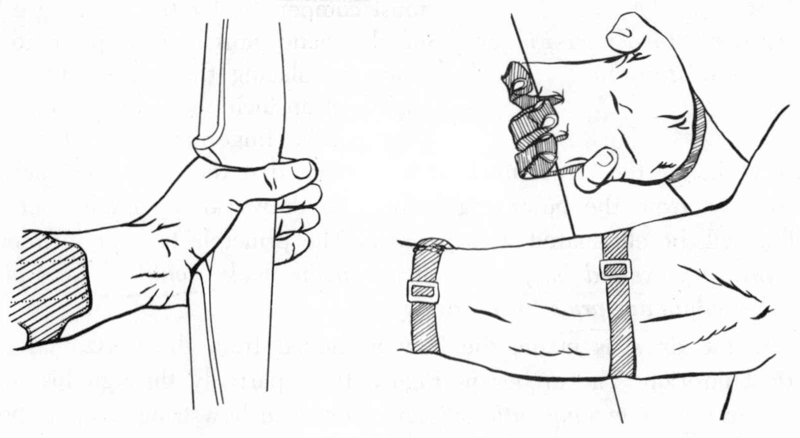

Figure 13—Bow Hold

Figure 14—Three Finger Grip

three fingers are placed on the bowstring at the level of the distal finger joints, i.e., the bowstring is placed in the crease formed by the first finger joints. The distal and middle joints of the three fingers are flexed as the draw is made. *It must be noted that the large knuckle joints of the hand are not flexed at any time during the draw.* In addition, the wrist is maintained in a straight or extended position throughout the draw and the release phases of the shot.

Figure 15 shows the relationship between the index and middle fingers and the nock of the arrow. Although this appears to be simple, position of the fingers on the bowstring next to the arrow nock is difficult to maintain as the pressure increases during the draw. The essence of the problem lies in the nature of the musculature within the hand. As fingers are flexed, it is natural for them to be drawn tightly together into a fist. This is fine for boxing, but it creates arrow flight problems in archery! Because the index and middle fingers are flexed and the pressure increases during the draw, the two fingers have a tendency to apply pressure on the nock of the arrow. Beginning archers find that the point of the arrow will wave around and fall completely off the arrow rest as the draw is made. This is caused by finger pressure on the arrow nock. The archer must compensate for the gripping effect of the hand musculature prior to his draw by placing the index finger one-eighth of an inch above the arrow nock. The middle finger is placed the same distance below the arrow nock. It may seem that the arrow will become disengaged from the bowstring before the draw can be made, but this feeling will be eliminated with practice. The principle to bear in mind is that *pressure exerted by fingers on the arrow nock should be kept at an absolute minimum prior to the draw.*

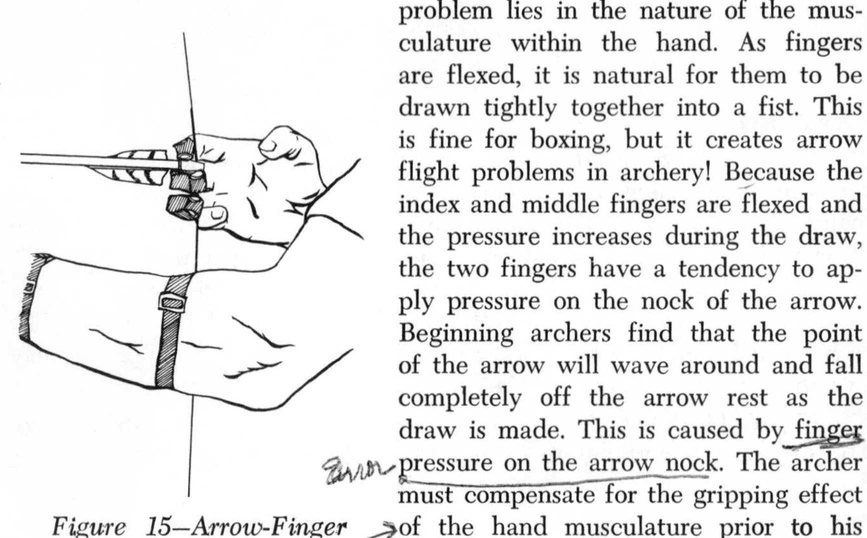

Figure 15—Arrow-Finger Relationship

As the draw is made, the bow is moved from the horizontal to a vertical position. The archer in Figure 16 is partially through his draw. *The bow arm is moving into full extension.* The bowstring hand is being pulled toward the face. As this is being done, the bow hand is relaxed from its hold on the bow and is used to push the bow as described previously. The completed draw is shown in Figure 17.

The position of the bow arm is very important. During the draw, the bow arm is raised to shoulder height. It should be extended or straight

Figure 16—Starting the Draw

Figure 17—Completed Draw

when the archer has drawn the arrow to his anchor point. (Some archers raise the bow arm higher than the shoulder and aim while moving the bow arm downward to shoulder height.)

The bowstring should not slap the bow arm after it has been released. The arm guard may be hit at times. This can be caused by such things as flinching, elbow and wrist movement. This is no cause for alarm, because "string slaps" will diminish as the archer increases in skill.

Some archers, however, do require adjustments of their shooting techniques to eliminate painful contusions caused by continued "string slaps" on the bow arm. If the bowstring hits the bow arm above the arm guard, the archer's stance should be opened a few inches. For most individuals, this will eliminate the problem. If a stance adjustment does not work, the archer should rotate his bow arm inward a few degrees at the shoulder —clockwise for a right-handed archer—while the total arm is extended. The bow hand is then supinated, turned counterclockwise, so the bow is in a vertical position. This will pull the arm out of the path of the bowstring.

What adjustments in arm position should be made to avoid string slap?

Evaluation Questions
AVOIDING STRING SLAP

Traditionally, authors have stated that a straight line should be drawn from the arrow point to the elbow of the drawing or bowstring arm. This is not the case in actual practice. Expert archers hold the elbow of the drawing arm slightly above the arrow shaft and arrow point. This elbow position is necessary to maintain a good arrow-finger relationship for the subsequent release.

ANCHOR POINT

The term "anchor point" means the place on an archer's face where he places his hand when he has the bowstring at full draw. Anchor points are usually described as being either low or high. An anchor point on or under the jaw bone is low. An anchor point on or under the bone under the eye is high. Preference usually involves such factors as facial contour and type of shooting. Many field archers, bow hunters and instinctive shooters use the high anchor point. Many of these archers like to think they sight down the shaft of the arrow but actually they look over the arrow point. The low anchor point is used very often by target archers who rely on bow sights for aiming. Both types can be used for any kind of shooting. The archer ultimately should use the anchor point which feels the most comfortable to him.

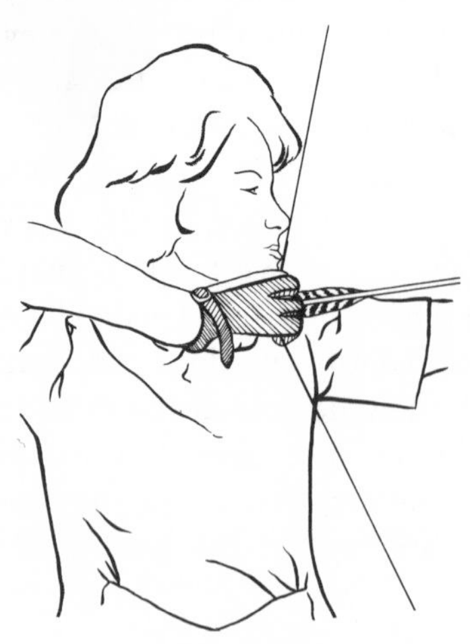

Figure 18—Low Anchor Point

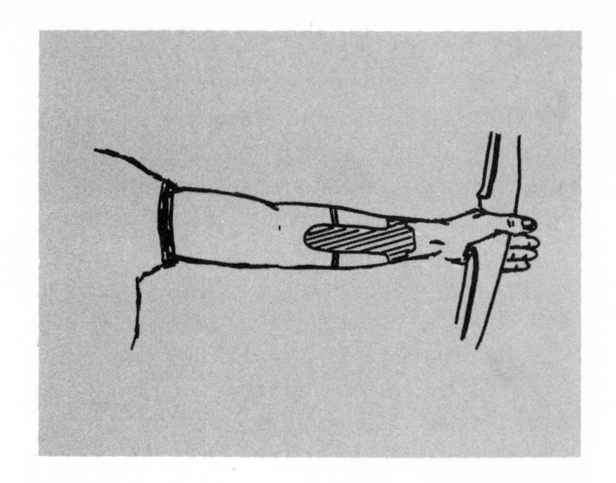

Diagram B:
AVOIDING STRING SLAP

An archer should try both styles of anchor points. It is recommended that the beginner use the high anchor point until he becomes adjusted to his tackle. To use the high anchor point, place the index finger of the bowstring hand next to the mouth. The knuckle of the index finger touches the zygomatic arch and the bowstring is aligned with the middle of the eye which is away from the target.

Figure 18 shows the low anchor point. For consistency, the beginner should practice with this anchor point as soon as he has had an opportunity to shoot several ends. To learn any athletic activity, one must utilize as many of his senses as possible. The low anchor point involves a good distribution of touch, pressure, sight and feeling. The index finger is placed under the chin. Slight pressure is exerted on the mandible. This position allows the bowstring to bisect and actually touch the chin, lips and nose. Some archers place rubber kissing buds on their bowstrings. These are "kissed" each time the low anchor is set. This practice insures maximum consistency in regard to the accurate placement of the archer's low anchor point.

Some beginning archers feel that they must change the anchor point and length of draw when shooting from greater distances. *The anchor point and draw remain constant for all distances.*

AIMING

Three aiming techniques are referred to rather frequently in archery literature: (1) bow sights, (2) instinctive and (3) point-of-aim. The bow sight technique should be mastered and used by the archer in all target archery tournaments. The instinctive technique has many limitations, especially in target archery tournaments and in bow hunting situations. The point-of-aim technique is antiquated and not recommended.

The beginner should not worry too much about any aiming procedure or technique until he feels comfortable with his tackle. When fundamentals have been learned, the archer may turn his attention to aiming and grouping of arrows in smaller and smaller patterns on the target.

The use of the bow sight will greatly enhance ability to hit the target. The archer must establish a bow sight setting on his bow for each shooting distance. This requires shooting a great number of ends at each distance. To use the bow sight, the archer places the sighting device in the middle of the intended target—the gold on a regulation target archery face—and releases the arrow. This procedure is repeated until several ends have been shot. The archer must continually check for grouping patterns on the target face. For example, an archer shoots six ends of arrows at a target without changing the bow sight setting. All arrows are grouped low and to the left on a regulation archery target face, i.e., the grouping is at seven o'clock in the black. The archer should move his bow sighting device down and to the left for his next series of shots. In other words, *the bow sight is moved in the direction of the arrow grouping error*. In our example, if the adjustment is correct and fundamentals are good, the next six ends should be grouped in or near the gold on the target face. Establishing bow sight settings requires considerable shooting and some degree of experimentation. *The archer must be fundamentally sound to expect good results from bow sight aiming.*

Many "experts" contend that the eye nearer the target should be closed during the act of shooting. This is a fallacy! What if the eye away from the target—the right eye for a right-handed archer—is the weak eye? Should he close his good eye and keep his weak eye open? Logically one would assume that this could have a detrimental bearing upon accuracy. Many fine right-handed archers shoot with both eyes open or with the left eye partially closed and the right eye open. Eye preference is a highly individualized matter. The beginner should try shooting while using all combinations of eye opening and closure. He should use the eye position which feels most comfortable to him. It is recommended that both eyes be open during the act of shooting if possible.

Sighting or aiming with a bow and arrow is not like aiming a rifle. The rifleman looks down the top of the rifle barrel through a series of sights mounted on the barrel. While using the low anchor point in particular, the archer does not and should not look down the shaft of his arrow. He should look through the aiming device on his bow sight. The bow sight is mounted *above* the arrow shaft. At a relatively close distance to a target, the actual line-of-sight may be from the eye through the arrow point to a point on the ground in front of the intended target. This principle was utilized in the older point-of-aim technique.

Many gun hunters, who find bow hunting challenging as a sport also, use the high anchor point. This offers them the opportunity to sight over the arrow point while aiming. This procedure is analogous to rifle aiming techniques, except the arrow point does not have a sight mounted on it. As a result, many bow hunters use what is commonly known as instinctive aiming techniques.

Bare bows, bows without sighting devices, are used extensively in field archery. Tournaments are held in field archery exclusively for so-called instinctive shooters. Many excellent scores are recorded in these tournaments, and the lack of mechanical aiming devices adds to the spirit of true sport. There are many strong arguments for the use of bare bows.

Each archer who uses instinctive aiming usually gives a slightly different version of how he accomplishes the task. For one thing, the instinctive archer must have excellent eyesight and depth perception. He does not have anything else to guide him. The term "instinct" as it is used in conjunction with this style of shooting is grossly incorrect. *Through extensive practice over a long period of time,* the archer increases his kinesthetic awareness, visual awareness and archery skills. (Instinct has little, if anything, to do with it!) This set of factors enables him to adjust rapidly as he peers over the arrow point toward the target. The archer sees a gap or space between the arrow point and the target. His release is calculated to coincide with the arrow point's bisection of the aiming area and his line-of-sight. The archer holds the bow arm motionless for a second at the time of release. The beginner should practice with the bow sight technique extensively prior to trying instinctive shooting. It is absolutely amazing what practice can do for one's instinct!

RELEASE

Releasing or loosing the arrow is probably the most important phase of shooting. The key factors are (1) relaxation and (2) concentration. The paradoxical nature of these two factors at this critical stage of shooting adds another dimension to the challenge of archery as a sport. As the reader knows, it is extremely difficult to relax during a time of intense concentration. Both must be done, however, to achieve any degree of success in archery.

How should the bow sight be adjusted if arrow grouping is consistent in this area? if it is down and to the right?

Evaluation Questions

ADJUSTING THE BOW SIGHT

Releasing an arrow *is not* a result of forceful finger extension. It *is* a matter of relaxing the musculature within the bow hand and forearm. When the muscles controlling flexion within the three drawing fingers relax, the bowstring will begin to move forward as a result of the pressure of the bow weight at complete draw. The bowstring will brush the fingers away from its path if they have been relaxed sufficiently. The archer does very little muscular work at the time of release. As already stated, his main problems are *relaxation* of hand and forearm muscles and maximum *concentration* prior to and at the time of release. It is too late to concentrate when the arrow is in flight!

Figure 19 shows proper release form. The elbow of the bowstring arm should not extend appreciably after or during the release. The bowstring hand may move backward in a position close to the chin or neck. This would be a natural recoil action. The beginner must avoid the habit of trying to release the arrow by hyperextending the wrist—moving the back of the hand toward the forearm and allowing the bowstring to roll off the finger tips. This causes very erratic arrow grouping.

Follow-through—Follow-through means holding the release position until the arrow is safely imbedded in the target (Figure 20).

The following are features of a good follow-through in archery: (1) the fingers on the bowstring hand are relaxed, (2) the head and eyes are turned toward the target, (3) the bow arm is extended toward the target and (4) the bow hand is gripping the bow. Why is follow-through important? It is absolutely essential for consistent performance.

Diagram C:
ADJUSTING THE BOW SIGHT

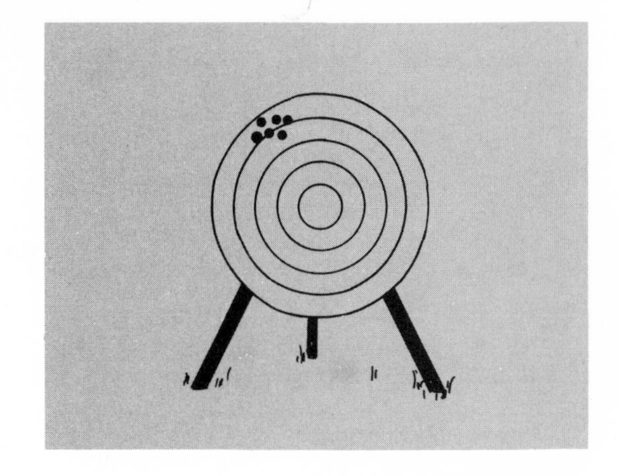

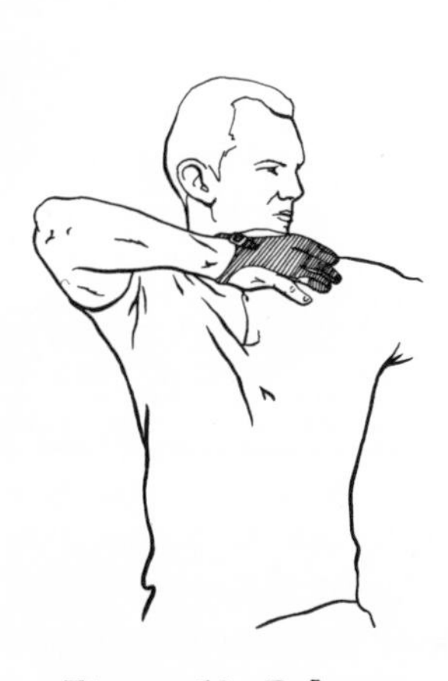

Figure 19—Release

Figure 20—Follow-through

SCORING

Figure 21 shows two archers retrieving and scoring their arrows. The target archery face most commonly used by beginning archers is 48 inches in diameter. It has five concentric rings which are colored gold (the center or bull's eye), red, blue, black and white. The point values are nine, seven, five, three and one respectively. A perfect end therefore is worth 54 points. A *round* consists of a designated number of ends shot at varying distances. Using baseball as an analogous example, an end would equal one inning and nine innings or a complete game would

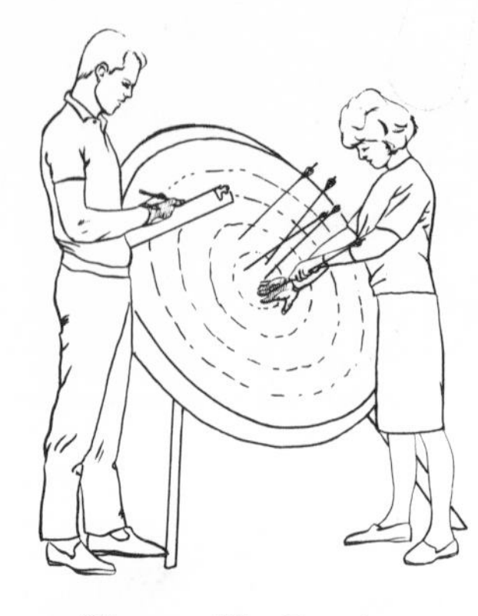

Figure 21–Scoring

equal a round. There are numerous standard rounds for all ages and both sexes. Some of these rounds are described in Chapter 3.

Scoring in target archery should be done by a target captain. This individual pulls the arrows from the target. The high value arrows are always pulled first. The target captain tells the score of the arrow to the recorder who marks the score on a score card. The recorder also indicates the number of hits on the score card.

Scoring of target archery has the following variations:

1. Arrows which pass completely through the target are given a value of seven points if they were shot from sixty yards or less.
2. Arrows which pass completely through the target are given five points if they were shot from more than 60 yards.
3. An arrow which bisects a line between colors is given the higher value of the two colors.
4. An arrow which rebounds from the target is scored seven points if shot from 60 yards or less and five points if shot from more than 60 yards.

Pulling arrows from a target mat mounted on a tripod stand should be done with caution. The arrow should be grasped by the shaft near the target face with one hand. The other hand should be used to push against the target mat while the arrow is pulled from the target. This simple procedure eliminates the embarrassing and costly experience of pulling a target full of arrows over onto the ground. No one should stand behind the person who is pulling arrows from a target.

3

Archery as a Sport

An archer may use his archery skills in many ways throughout his lifetime. Several phases of archery as a sport are described in this chapter. The sport of bow hunting is discussed separately in Chapter 4.

TARGET ARCHERY

For competitive purposes, the National Archery Association classifies archers by age and sex as follows:

1. *Beginner* boys and girls—eleven years of age and under
2. *Junior* boys and girls—twelve to fourteen years of age
3. *Intermediate* boys and girls—fifteen to seventeen years of age
4. *Ladies*—seventeen years of age and older
5. *Men*—seventeen years of age and older

There are recognized target rounds for each of these classifications. A few of the more popular rounds used in national tournament competition are discussed in this section.

The *American Round* is for ladies, men and intermediate archers. Five ends are shot at 60, 50, and 40 yards respectively, with the greatest distance being shot first for any target archery round. This amounts to a total of 90 arrows for the round and a potential score of 810. An American Round score of 630 to 680 for a college student in an archery class is considered good. Competitive men archers shoot American Round scores consistently above 750 points. Scores by ladies are above 700, and the national winner's score will exceed 700 points by a comfortable margin.

The *Junior American Round* is for junior boys and girls. It consists of five ends from the 50, 40 and 30 yard lines respectively. This is a good skills test round for beginning archers after one school semester of shooting. The beginner should set 600 as his basic goal for this round, an average of 40 points per end.

The *Columbia Round* for ladies consists of shooting four ends from the 50, 40 and 30 yard lines respectively. The maximum score is 648. Ladies who shoot competitively at the national level make scores near 600. The winners will exceed 600 points.

The *York Round* for men is extremely difficult. It consists of shooting twelve ends from 100 yards, eight ends from 80 yards and four ends from 60 yards. To gain some insight into the difficulty of this round, it is recommended that the beginning archer try shooting a few ends over these distances after he becomes familiar with tackle and shooting techniques. This experience would add to his appreciation of the skill levels attained by some of the better archers in the world. The potential score for the York Round is 1,296 points. The 1,000 point total can be a barrier for the York Round, but it has been shot on many occasions. An average of seven points per arrow is excellent for experienced archers at the difficult distances of the York Round.

The *National Round* for ladies consists of eight ends from sixty yards and six ends from fifty yards. The potential score is 648 points. A good competitive archer will do well if she shoots above 570 points. A good goal for relatively inexperienced archers at the college level is between 475 and 500 points.

There are also *Team Rounds* for each shooting classification. A team in target archery consists of four archers. The scores of the four team members are combined for the team score. The Team Round for men consists of sixteen ends shot from 60 yards, and for women sixteen ends shot from 50 yards. A good score for each team member in a beginning college class in archery is in the 650 to 675 point range. Men and women archers in national tournaments shoot individual scores near the 750 point mark. The team winner will have scores near the 800 mark made by each of the four team members.

The international archery organization is known as the *Federation Internationale De Tir A L'Arc* or *F.I.T.A.* The rounds sanctioned by the F.I.T.A. are shot at distances from 90 to 30 meters. The 48 inch target face is used only at the 90, 70 and 60 meter ranges. A .80 meter target face is used at 50 and 30 meters. Scoring also differs for international competition. Each color area on the two target faces is divided in its center by a ring. Consequently, scoring from the center ring outward is 10 and 9 (gold); 8 and 7 (red); 6 and 5 (blue); 4 and 3 (black); and

Evaluation Questions

Can you name the national organizations which govern archery in the United States? What are their official publications?

2 and 1 (white). This scoring procedure applies to both target faces. Men shoot six ends from 90, 70, 50 and 30 meters respectively. Women shoot six ends from 70, 60, 50, and 30 meters respectively. In the world target championships two of these complete rounds must be shot for total score. The good international archers, men and women, consistently exceed 1,000 points per round.

CLOUT SHOOTING

Clout shooting is a form of target archery sanctioned by the National Archery Association. It is not as popular today as it was several years ago. There are clout rounds for each shooting classification:

1. *Ladies*—140 and 120 yards
2. *Men*—180 yards
3. *Junior Boys and Intermediate Girls*—120 yards
4. *Junior Girls, Beginner Boys and Beginner Girls*—80 yards.

Thirty-six arrows are shot during each round at a specific distance.

So that the reader does not become alarmed at the great distances which are shot by ladies and men, it should be noted that the target face for a clout round is much larger than the regulation target archery face. The target consists of a series of concentric circles exactly like the target archery face; however, instead of the outer circle being 48 inches in diameter it is 48 *feet* in diameter. The target rings are made by burning or marking lines on the grass. The center of the middle ring is marked with a small flag on a five foot pole. The archers shoot from a shooting line which can not exceed 50 yards in length.

Clout shooting is challenging and fascinating. The archer must have good depth perception to become skilled. He must also have excellent kinesthetic acuity to assist him as he aims, i.e., he must be able to feel exactly when the bow arm is at the proper angle from his body prior to release of the arrow. A prism sighting device can be used in clout shooting.

Scoring a clout round is exactly the same as scoring one of the National Archery Association rounds mentioned previously. Arrows, which must stick within the target area, are given the point value of the ring in which they fall. A score in the 250 to 275 point range for a clout round is considered good if shot by a novice archer. Experienced clout shooters score near 300.

Field archers have a traditional clout round known as the *Battle Clout*. The shooting distance for this round is 200 yards. The bull's eye ring has a twelve foot diameter. The remaining rings are laid out in concentric fashion, six feet apart. The outermost ring for the Battle Clout is 60 feet in diameter.

The field archer shooting in the Battle Clout must use a broadhead arrow point. The arrow may not weigh less than 425 grains. This form of shooting originated in the many battles which were fought by archers throughout history, especially the classic battles between the English and French during the Hundred Years' War. The archers shot great volleys of arrows into the air in clout fashion toward their opponents. This was an early and effective form of aerial bombardment. The reader can understand the apprehension of an entrenched soldier as a volley of thousands of arrows suddenly descends into his area. In addition to being an effective killing technique, the battle clout also caused panic on many occasions.

FIELD ARCHERY

The organization which controls field archery in several countries is known as the *National Field Archery Association, N.F.A.A.* Field archery is actually an outgrowth of target archery. The main difference lies in the fact that field archery ranges usually are constructed in rugged terrain. The archer must move from target to target in a fashion which is analogous to the golfer moving from hole to hole on a golf course.

Unlike the target archer, the field archer commonly uses the bare bow and instinctive shooting techniques. Field archers who use bow sights or aiming devices are placed in a free style division for competitive purposes. Instinctive shooters do not compete against free style shooters in N.F.A.A. tournaments. Many people believe that the field archer shoots at moving targets during a round, but field archery targets are stable and are not automated during a round. The archer must move to a designated shooting area for each target.

The *Field Round* has twenty-eight different shooting positions or targets which vary in size depending upon their distances from the shooting line. As examples, the archer may shoot at a six inch target from a distance of 20 feet; a 12 inch target from a distance of 20 yards; an 18 inch target from 50 yards and a 24 inch target from 65 yards. The target face for the Field Round consists of a white center ring with a black spot. The black spot can be used to assist the archer with his aiming. A hit in the white area is worth five points. The outer circle is black and a hit in that area is worth three points. Four arrows are used in the Field Round.

The *Hunter's Round* is also shot over a field range. The target is all black with a white aiming spot in its center. A fine white line separates the inner from the outer circle. The scoring is the same as for the Field Round. The course is laid out so the archer shoots over a cumulative total of 980 yards.

The *Big Game Round* has 28 shooting positions. Life-sized animal target faces are used. The bull's eye area is directly over the heart or a vital organ of the animal. A hit in the remainder of the scoring area would usually mean a kill if the animal were alive when shot. The archer is allowed to shoot three arrows at each target if needed. A bull's eye with the first arrow scores 20 points, and a hit in the scoring ring outside the bull's eye scores 15 points. A bull's eye with the second arrow scores 15 points, and a hit within the scoring ring outside the bull's eye scores 10 points. A bull's eye with the third arrow scores 10 points, and a hit within the scoring ring is worth 5 points. A scoring hit with any arrows at any target terminates the shooting at that target position. If an archer misses with all three arrows, no score is recorded. In both instances, three misses or a hit, the archer retrieves his arrow(s) and moves to the next animal target.

FLIGHT SHOOTING

Flight shooting is the sport of shooting arrows for maximum distance. These events are conducted under the auspices of the National Archery Association. Restrictions for competition are based primarily on bow weights and secondarily on the age and sex classifications mentioned

What is the score for this hit during a Field Round?

Evaluation Questions

SCORING A FIELD ROUND HIT

previously. Each age and sex division has an unlimited weight and foot bow class. (A foot bow has a heavy draw which requires the archer to lie on his back and draw the string with both hands while pushing the belly of the bow with his feet—pedominal shooting.)

The distances attained by expert flight shooters with excellent flight shooting tackle is phenomenal. It is not unusual for a distance of 500 yards to be attained by youngsters, and distances of 700 yards are not impossible for men. The key factor in flight shooting is arrow velocity. Flight tackle is designed for this specific purpose. As a result, a flight bow may project an arrow some 50 to 60 feet per second faster than a target archery bow. A flight shooter is shown in Figure 22.

WAND SHOOTING

Wand Shooting dates back at least to sixteenth century England. The wand stands six feet high and is two inches in width. Thirty-six arrows are used for wand rounds. Hits as well as rebounds are scored. The distances for wand shooting follow:

1. *Men*—100 yards
2. *Intermediate Boys*—80 yards
3. *Ladies and Intermediate Girls*—60 yards
4. *Junior Boys*—50 yards
5. *Junior Girls and Beginner Boys*—40 yards
6. *Beginner Girls*—30 yards

Figure 22—Flight Shooting

There is a legendary report of a wand shoot between Robin Hood and another character named

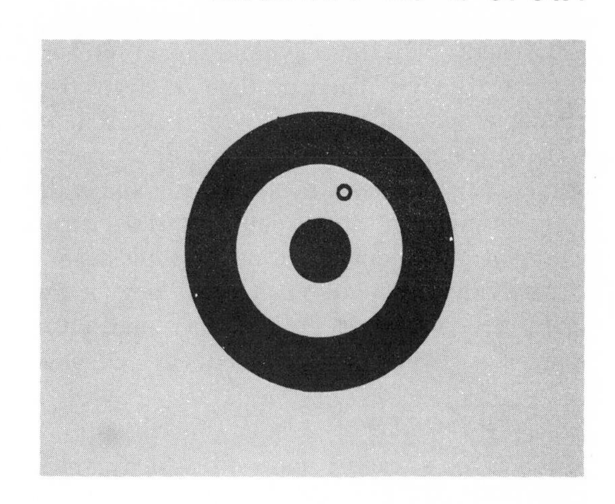

Diagram D:
SCORING A FIELD ROUND HIT

Clifton. According to the tale, Clifton shot his arrow first and it hit the two inch wand at 100 yards. Before Clifton's arrow stopped oscillating, Robin Hood released his arrow and it completely split the shaft of Clifton's vibrating arrow! The mathematical probability of the occurrence of such an event is fantastic. Even with excellent modern tackle it is highly improbable that such a feat could occur. The best contemporary trick shot archers usually make their shots at distances of 10 to 20 yards. Some movie stunt men do not rely on skill alone for those close-up shots of arrows "penetrating" a human body. Many times an arrow is mounted on wire and guided directly to its mark where it actually penetrates a large pad which is strategically placed under the stunt man's clothing. Such procedures make the story of Robin Hood's wand shot more fantastic.

THE OLYMPIC GAMES

There was a great effort made around the world to have archery included for the first time in the 1964 Olympic Games held in Tokyo, Japan. These efforts failed, but archery will be an Olympic sport in the 1972 Olympic Games. During the 1968 Games, which will be held in Mexico City, Mexico, the world's best archers will compete on an unofficial or demonstration basis.

Many of the best archers in America could not compete on an Olympic Team because they are considered to be professionals by Amateur Athletic Union and Olympic standards. Many have engaged in money tournaments. It has not been uncommon in the past for winning archers to receive trophies, merchandise or credit worth more than forty dollars. Any one of these acts is enough to cause an archer to lose his amateur status.

ARCHERY AS A SPORT

Where will the Olympic Team archers come from for the 1972 Olympic Games? There is time to develop good archers. With good instruction and diligent practice, a person can develop into a potential archery champion of national and international caliber within a period of one to two years. A person of any age with the proper attitude, interest, aptitude and motivation could possibly earn a position on the team. To represent one's country on an Olympic team is one of the highest honors an individual can attain. This is now a possibility for archers for the first time in history. It is proper and fitting that one of man's oldest sports has finally been added to the Olympic sports agenda.

ARCHERY GOLF

This is a casual sport in which archers can be matched against golfers. It also can be played by archers only. Archery golf combines aspects of flight shooting, clout shooting and field archery primarily. It is played on a regular golf course or can be played on a simulated golf course. The "hole" or target consists of a twelve inch ball made of soft material mounted on a short stick. The target should be on or near the golf green. The preference of the operators of the golf course usually determines target placement. Sometimes they are not too receptive to the idea of having arrows imbedded in well kept golf greens. The target should have four and eight inch rings painted on it. To start the match, the archer flight or clout shoots from the regulation golf tee area toward the golf green. All "putting" shots are made from a distance of at least ten yards from the target. A hit within the four inch ring on the target *adds* one point only to the archer's score; a hit within the eight inch ring raises the archer's score by two points. A hit outside the eight inch ring raises the score by three points. As in golf, the low score over 18 holes wins.

Let us follow one archer for one hole. He is shooting a five par, 500 yard hole. His first shot from the tee carries 300 yards. The second shot lands within twenty yards of the target. The archer's third shot imbeds itself in the inner ring of the target. One point is added to the number of shots required to reach the target. Our archer's score is four or a birdie for the hole, i.e., one under par. Archery golf is played primarily as a novelty sport.

MAIL MATCHES

Many schools and clubs compete in rounds where the archers do not leave their home ranges. Scores are mailed or phoned to a tournament chairman at the host school or club. When the scores have been processed the results are mailed to the competing teams. Individual and team scores are listed, and tournament records are kept up to date from one year to the next. Generally, these rounds are conducted on an annual basis. As an example, Arizona State University at Tempe, Arizona, sponsors a mail match annually which involves college and university archers throughout the United States. Mail matches help to stimulate interest in competitive archery.

The Olympic Bowman League in Chicago sponsors mail matches. There are two official rounds for adults: (1) *The Olympic Round*—15 ends are shot from 30 yards at the official N.A.A. target and (2) the *Chicago Round*—16 ends are shot from 20 yards at a target which has a diameter of 16 inches.

BOW FISHING

Bow fishing is growing in popularity. Special tackle is required if the archer wants to try his hand at this sport. Fishing arrow points are designed in many shapes and forms (Figure 4). A barbed arrow point is essential. Bow fishing arrow shafts are made of plastic, wood and aluminum. They do not need the precise workmanship required for target archery arrows. Rubber vanes are used instead of feathers. The arrow should be relatively heavy because it must travel through water for some distance prior to hitting the fish. Not all fish accommodate the archer by swimming on top or by jumping out of the water! Bow fishing reels are designed to satisfy any individual preference. They range from ultra-automatic to hand-winding designs.

Bow fishing can be more challenging than any other form of archery. The difficulties of conquering the basic fundamentals of archery are compounded by the water and other natural forces. Consider the plight of a bow fisherman in a rowboat or canoe on a river or lake. The wind is mild and the water is disturbed slightly. The boat is rocking a bit as the game fish is sighted. First, the archer must stand in the boat to position himself for the shot. One of his major problems commences as he tries to aim while weaving from side to side to maintain his own upright posture. In addition, he finds that shooting at a fish is different from shooting at a land target. The land target does not have water in front of it to distort his view of the target! The archer must calculate the refraction of the sun's light rays as they penetrate the water in the area of his fish. Furthermore, the actual depth of the fish is deceptive to the naked eye, because the light rays have a tendency to bend downward. The archer

Where would an archer see a target of this type?

Evaluation Questions
IDENTIFYING THE TARGET

must aim at an area in front of the fish if he is to have any chance of hitting it, because fish will not hold still for any appreciable length of time! Thus our bow fisherman has his problems, but *these problems are what makes this aspect of archery a sport*. The bow fisherman can derive considerable personal satisfaction when he overcomes these problems and places his fish in the creel.

States have different laws regarding bow fishing. Bow fishing and spearing are usually placed in the same category when legislative action is considered. The bow fisherman should check his local fish and game laws to be certain regarding bow fishing regulations in his area of the United States. These laws change periodically. Generally, however, carp, gar and catfish can be taken with the bow and arrow in most states. Ocean fishing sometimes requires a professional fishing license for the bow fisherman.

Some readers may say that bow fishing for carp and catfish is too mild. They like a little more adventure in their sport. As stated previously, archery provides something of interest for almost everyone. Perhaps *bow fishing for alligators* would satisfy a desire for challenge and adventure! Alligator can be taken with the bow and arrow on a limited scale in Texas and Georgia. Again, game laws should be checked annually. Landing a 400-pound alligator with a bow and arrow presents problems of a different magnitude than landing a ten-pound catfish.

INDOOR ARCHERY LANES

Indoor archery lanes were first introduced at the World's Fair in Seattle, Washington. Since that time, they have slowly increased in number in some of the larger cities, particularly those on the Pacific Coast.

Diagram E:
IDENTIFYING THE TARGET

Automated, indoor archery lanes are similar to bowling lanes in appearance and operation. Targets are set on an automatic device in a lane. The archer may set his target at the desired distance automatically. Following the shooting of an end or any number of arrows, the archer presses a button and the target moves to the archer. Arrows are pulled and scores are recorded. The target is then returned to the desired shooting distance. For the use of the target and tackle, the archer pays an hourly rental fee. Indoor archery lanes have stimulated interest in archery. Many local and professional tournaments are held within these facilities.

Archery is one of the fastest growing sports in America. There are activities for virtually all interests. The individual who is interested in earning money as a professional archer will find that there is an increasing number of tournaments where winners earn cash, many with prizes in excess of $10,000. There is a decided relationship between professional archery today and the status of professional golf and bowling twenty years ago. There is no reason to believe that archery will not grow in much the same way.

The amateur will find an increasing number of opportunities to use his archery skills in recreational settings in his community. Many large corporations, for example, are starting archery as a sport within their employee recreation programs. Regardless of an individual's economic status, locale or skill level, archery can be engaged in as a sport in some meaningful form.

Bow Hunting

Hunting with the bow and arrow has grown a great deal in popularity during the past decade. Deer is usually the first type of game animal which comes to mind when the subject of bow hunting is discussed, but game animals are as numerous for the bow as for the gun hunter. As examples, one may bow hunt for squirrel, quail, coyote, wild boar, fox, bob cat, lion and bear. Each animal presents a different set of problems. Many of these same problems do not exist for the gun hunter, because a man with a powerful gun can compensate for his lack of hunting skill through his weapon's ability. The bow hunter can not do this. The bow hunter must be a *hunter* in every sense of the word. Because hunting is actually more of an art with the bow than with a gun, bow hunting has increased in popularity.

TACKLE

If the archer chooses good tackle he can use it for most forms of archery with some slight modifications. The principles for purchasing hunting tackle are virtually the same as those for buying target archery tackle.

A 35 to 45 pound recurve bow can be used by most men for hunting. (It should be noted that some states place a 40 pound limit on hunting bows.) This is sufficient to provide the force needed to kill most game animals in North America. A 50 to 70 pound bow would be safer, however, for use against big game such as grizzly bear. A lady interested in bow hunting would purchase a lighter bow. Most skilled women archers of average strength can handle a 25 to 35 pound bow very efficiently, and this is enough poundage to kill most game animals.

The arrows for hunting must differ slightly from those used in target and field archery. Aluminum shafts are recommended. The aluminum arrow assures the archer of the greatest accuracy. Why spend considerable time and expense on a hunting trip and miss your game due to cheap, inaccurate arrows? The aluminum arrow can handle the heavier hunting arrow point better than wooden or fiberglass arrows. To add to arrow stability with the larger hunting point, the fletching should be lengthened to five or six inches. The arrow shaft should not be painted forest green or some other color for camouflage purposes but should be white or yellow. The bright color will reduce the number of lost arrows and will not "spook" the game animal once the arrow is in flight. Finally, hunting arrows, like target arrows, must be matched in all respects.

The arrow points for hunting are designed to kill game by two techniques: (1) hemorrhage and (2) impact. The arrow points designed to kill by hemorrhage *must be razor sharp* to be most effective. It is important to remember that an arrow point which is dull will not always kill an animal, because the blood vessels will not be lacerated to allow a steady, unobstructed blood flow. The dull arrow point will tear instead of cutting. A torn vein often will constrict to act as its own protective mechanism against hemorrhage. The bow hunter who is attempting to kill does not want this to occur. An archer shooting a dull arrow must strike a vital organ to kill his game, but this is not necessarily true if a razor sharp arrow is used. Such a hit in a large muscle group, for example, will clearly sever arteries, veins, capillaries and other blood vessels in the area causing hemorrhage sufficient and fast enough to result in death rather quickly. The bow hunter merely has to follow the stricken animal's trail until it collapses from asphyxiation. Most large animals are taken by using the hemorrhage technique.

The impact technique is used on small animals such as squirrel and rabbit. A blunt arrow point is used, a hard rubber tip that is slipped over or glued to the arrow shaft. The shock of the blunted arrow is usually enough to cause death instantly regardless of the point of impact on the animal. The blunt point would not be recommended for use on a charging grizzly bear except by those more adventurous hunters.

Some bow hunters like to make special adjustments on their bows for the hunting season. Doug Kittredge, a leading archery expert, camouflages his bow by painting it forest green. He also tapes an extra bowstring to the bow in case the one in use breaks or becomes inefficient. It is also a good idea to attach brush buttons or string silencers to the bowstring. These are simple rubber devices which tend to reduce the noise of the string vibrating and slapping the belly of the bow after the shot. A bow sight should be mounted on the bow with calibrated settings for short distances of 10, 20, 30 and 40 yards.

The length of the bow for hunting is a very important consideration. In the past many archers believed that a short bow length, 58 to 62 inches, was more desirable for hunting than any other length. Their argument usually centered around the fact that the shorter bow was less cumbersome in heavily wooded and foliaged areas. This may be true, but how many times does a good hunter confine himself to hunting in heavy brush? It is virtually impossible to shoot accurately under those circumstances with any length bow! The arrow will strike limbs and leaves and it will not find its mark because of deflections and loss of speed. A good hunter does not linger long in heavy brush. A more serious and negative factor of the short bow is the sharp angle which is created where the archer grips the bowstring and the arrow. This angle at the nocking point tends to compress the fingers of the bowstring hand so tightly that a smooth release is very difficult, especially for the individual who has not shot the short bow extensively. A longer bow, 64 to 70 inches, has longer limbs and a longer bowstring; consequently, the angle created at the nocking area at full draw is greater than the same angle for the short bow. This allows a smoother release. A bow length of 64 to 66 inches for multipurpose bows is recommended if the draw length is 28 inches.

TECHNIQUES

The bow hunter needs to train and condition himself prior to the hunting season in order to perfect his timing and accuracy and to put himself in good general condition.

Practice on a target is essential. If the archer has been shooting with target or field points, he should switch to heavier broadheads or hunting points for his preseason practice. The flight patterns of the arrow equipped with broadheads will be different, and he will need to adjust his bow sight for the distances of his choice.

Muscles will have to be conditioned for bow hunting, especially if the hunter has been sedentary for several weeks or months. Shooting a bow and arrow when fatigued is vastly different from shooting when rested. The bow hunter may get his best shot of the year when he is very tired. He should know how to compensate for this feeling when he shoots. The best way to accomplish this is to practice shooting when fatigued as well as rested. The bow hunter should walk over considerable distances daily prior to the hunting season. This will help develop minimal muscular endurance in the legs. Walking alone, however, is not enough for condi-

Evalution Questions

Using the formula: $S = 1/2\ at^2$ (S = distance; a = gravity; t = time in seconds) how far above the target must an arrow be aimed to make nine points if you are shooting with a bow that imparts the arrow at 100 feet per second from 30 yards? with a bow that imparts the arrow at 200 feet per second?

tioning purposes. Jogging for a continuous period of twenty minutes daily is recommended for developing cardiovascular and muscular endurance. If this regimen is followed, no terrain will be too difficult for the bow hunter.

All shots made in the field will not be like shots made on the target range; consequently, it is a good idea to practice on a field archery range. The good bow hunter practices on target and field archery ranges by taking shots while in unusual positions. One should practice shooting from the knees, standing on the side of a hill and shooting with the bow held at various angles ranging from vertical to horizontal positions. The terrain of the hunting field is usually very unlike the terrain of a target archery range.

The bow hunter should practice judging distances constantly. This can be done almost anywhere. As an example, while walking pick out a sign, tree, person or object and estimate its distance. Then count your steps as you move toward the object. Judgment of distance will improve steadily through such practice. Why is this important to the bow hunter? If he uses a bow sight as recommended, it will help him gauge his distance more precisely in the hunting environment. This, logically, can lead to more game.

Like the Indian of yesteryear, the bow hunter must know his game. He must know their eating and drinking habits, and he should know about their habitat. It is a good idea to go into the hunting area on foot a few weeks prior to the hunting season if possible to study or scout the intended game. For example, a deer herd may be observed for several days. Their eating, drinking and bedding habits can be seen. Some men are so good at this that they actually choose the deer to be shot prior to the opening of the season. This takes patience, knowledge and skill. Many hunters of the "instant hunting school" are in such a hurry to get their game that they fail to enjoy the hunt. One misses a great deal when he drives through back country roads in an automobile looking for wild game!

An important part of any hunt is the fine art of stalking or seeking out the game animals. This is more important in bow than gun hunting, because the bow hunter must get closer to the game animal. Most deer, for example, are killed with the bow and arrow at distances ranging from 20 to 40 yards, and the deer are usually standing still when shot. To get this type of shot, the bow hunter must be a good stalker with intimate knowledge of deer. Stalking involves knowledge of the game animal, noises and scents in the area; wind direction changes by time of day; animal camouflage and animal movements.

Noise can be used to the bow hunter's advantage. Many hunters believe that they should be absolutely quiet at all times. This is not always the case. For one thing, it is virtually impossible to be quiet in some hunting situations. There is a great sport associated with bow hunting which actually depends upon noise. It is known as *varmint calling.* This is a sport where noise is used to attract predatory animals. The predator hears the noise made by the hunter. The game animal becomes the stalker and the hunter actually becomes the hunted object. This can be very exciting, especially when the predator is in the big cat family!

The varmint caller uses a hand built or commercially built device to attract the predator. The sound of the call is not like that emitted by any particular animal; however, it does resemble the squeal of many animals when in distress. This noise attracts the predator, because he associates the crying sound with previous experiences where he has obtained a meal. When the predator gets within a few feet of the area where the bow hunter is camouflaged, the hunter looses his arrow. The distance of the shot depends largely upon the hunter's courage. Some varmint callers are good enough to kill their intended victims with baseball bats! Animal calls work very effectively on the carnivorous, predatory animals, but they are relatively ineffective on such animals as deer and elk.

Noise that is not typical of the environment should be avoided as much as possible when stalking; however, noise can be used to flush game out of thick brushy areas. This usually panics the animals and causes them to move rapidly in several directions. A shot at such a time is usually unwise. The animal's trail would have to be followed with the hope of getting a good shot at a later time. Talking and noises associated with human beings should be avoided. A broken twig may alarm the animal, but animals in a wooded area are familiar with such noise. They will usually respond by looking intently in the direction of the sound. The best thing to do following such a noise is to remain motionless for a few minutes. A grazing animal will usually return to eating after he has assured himself that one of his predators is not in the area.

The bow hunter must also face one fact prior to stalking game animals. Regardless of cleanliness, his body has odors which are not typical of the hunting area. These odors come from his skin, breath, hair and human habits such as the use of tobacco and liquor. If the hunter does not hunt into the air currents, he is in real trouble. Every animal will know that a predator, man in this case, is in the area. The hunter should try to eliminate all odors of civilization. This can be done, in part, through study of wind patterns. Wind patterns differ depending upon the time of day and the nature of the terrain. Odors from the hunter should be eliminated by using pine scented soap, and refraining from the use of tobacco and liquor while on the hunt.

It may seem obvious, but the bow hunter must know how to see the animal being sought. This takes considerable practice and experience. In their natural habitat animals are capable of hiding or camouflaging themselves very effectively. The untrained eye can miss seeing a potential shot. Some animals, especially birds such as pheasant and quail, depend upon their cover and camouflage for protection even more than their movement abilities. There are no secrets for spotting game animals. The bow hunter should know the coloring of the animal he is hunting and how these colors change with the seasons. He should train himself to look for minute details any time he walks through a forest, wooded area or field. This practice will develop his visual acuity. There is no substitute for practice.

For the individual who likes to hunt, bow hunting can provide many worthwhile leisure hours. The game can be as small as a quail or as large as an elephant. The environment can range from the wilderness areas of Canada to the deserts of Southwest America. Bow hunting is for the adventurous individual who respects nature, sport and himself as a sportsman.

The Evolution of Archery

The history and significance of archery, if known completely, would fill an encyclopedia. A few selected historical events are discussed here. A toxophilite, an archery historian, could add much more.

Archery skill was of vital importance for thousands of years. It provided a means for survival and thus played a prominent role in the development of mankind. It may have been as important in this respect as the development of the wheel, fire and speech. Ancient man certainly learned how to use the bow and arrow effectively. If today's student had to depend upon his archery skill for personal protection and for securing food, his skill would be dramatically accelerated. A semester grade does not have the same motivational impact as survival!

Archery feats, depicted by ancient artists in primitive cave drawings, can be seen in Spain and France. Ancient sculptors carved archer warriors in Egypt to honor them and their feats. The bow is known to have been used by primitive tribes throughout the world as a musical instrument. Many theologians and toxophilites believe that David's Biblical harp was his bow. The bow can be plucked much like a bass violin and the harp.

Archery feats have given rise to many myths. The mythology of Greece, for example, includes archery feats by such famous characters as Apollo, Diana, Hercules and Eros. The English had Robin Hood and some contend that he actually lived. If so, his legendary feats with the bow and arrow tend to border on the mythological. Far Eastern ancient cultures were not without their Robin Hood counterparts.

Archery feats have played many roles in religious ceremonies. The Assyrians concluded a ritual by shooting an arrow toward the sun. The same type of ritual, the sun vow, was practiced by Indians on the southwest plains of America many centuries later. The Zen Buddhists place

Evaluation Questions

Do you know why archery skill was important to the English during the Fourteenth century?

great value on archery. It is advocated because of the meeting of the "mind" and the "soul" at the time of release. There are times when advocates of that religion hold the bow at full draw for many hours until they feel that there is a unification between the "mind" and "soul."

Man's ability to use the bow and arrow has changed the course of history on several occasions. Governments have been toppled and wars have been won because one side had superior archers, superior tackle or both. Let us look at a few of these events chronologically.

UPPER PALEOLITHIC PERIOD

It is virtually impossible to pinpoint when man started using bows and arrows. From artifacts such as arrow points and tools believed to have been used in making tackle, toxophilites generally agree that man started using crude archery tackle some time during the upper paleolithic period, 10,000 to 20,000 years ago.

Drawings in caves, believed to have been inhabited by Cro-Magnon man, depict archers hunting for wild game with fairly sophisticated bows and arrows. It is logical to assume that archery tackle must have been in use many centuries prior to the time of Cro-Magnon man. Carbon testing techniques of stone artifacts tend to give credence to this assumption.

Bows of any great age have not been found, because wood deteriorates rapidly. The oldest extant bows date back to 2,000 B.C. These were found in the drier climate of the Nile River Valley.

5000 B.C.

The Egyptians were able to free themselves from the Persians during this era. They became superior archers through diligent practice and this proved to be most important in battle. Spears, slingshots and slings probably were the primary weapons of war prior to the refinement of the bow and arrow.

1000 B.C.

The Persians moved to the area north and east of the Black and Caspian Seas to battle the Scythians. Each had trained archers as foot soldiers. The mounted archers of the Persians, however, proved to be too much for the Scythians and added another dimension to the use of archery skills during time of war; this technique was used by other military men throughout history.

850-950 A.D.

Charlemagne and his Vikings made things miserable for the English during a portion of this period. The key factor was the strategy used in many of the attacks. During amphibious assaults, not unlike those used by the Americans and Japanese during World War II, the archers launched great clouts or volleys of arrows into their intended target area—an early form of naval bombardment—prior to storming ashore. Thus, another dimension was added to the use of archery skills in war.

1066 A.D.

The Norman archers taught the English a long-lasting lesson at the Battle of Hastings. They literally faked the English out into the open. The Normans planned and executed a false retreat designed to draw the English archers out of their hiding places to pursue the fleeing Normans. When the English came into the open they were slaughtered. The English were superior archers and probably would have won if the false retreat had not been successful. The English remembered this lesson, and they used the same kind of tactics on the French some 300 years later at the Battle of Poitiers.

A famous tapestry, The Bayeux Tapestry, was embroidered by the women who remained behind. The band of linen is twenty inches wide and 231 feet long. Various aspects of the Battle of Hastings were portrayed on the tapestry.

1220 A.D.

Genghis Khan, another war leader who utilized mounted archers effectively, like the Persians placed his "Golden Horde" on horseback. This mobility and disrespect for human life allowed Genghis Khan to capture territory from the Pacific Ocean to the Volga River, and from the Caspian Sea to Northern Siberia.

1252 A.D.

It was at this time that the English established the long bow as their national weapon, a surprising fact for recurve bow designs were known by the English bowyers or bow makers. Recurve bows had been in use for centuries. A series of sculps, dated 490-480 B.C., from the Temple of Aigina depicts archers using highly sophisticated recurve bows. Since this design is superior, why did the English choose the long bow as their national weapon though they used it effectively? One hypothesis has been advanced in explanation. The recurve bow must be made of a composite of materials glued together. England is a damp country and the crude glues used at that time were not durable. Consequently, the bow would fall apart when put to use. If this were the case, the results would have been very embarrassing and dangerous in the middle of a battle! Recurve bows were used very effectively in drier, arid areas.

1340-1363 A.D.

This period marked the start of the rise of English archery superiority. The Hundred Years' War was getting underway with France. The first of the big encounters was the Battle of Crecy, 1346 A.D. The English used their archers in a wedge formation; this and their superior skill with the bow and arrow enabled them to slaughter the majority of the French archers.

It was during this time that Edward III of England declared that archery had to be practiced, and that all other sports were illegal. This government edict had a direct effect on the level of skill of the entire population. It would be analogous to a president of the United States passing a law requiring everyone to practice daily with the latest model of the infantryman's rifle.

The Battle of Poitier took place in 1356 A.D. Although the English warriors were outnumbered more than two to one, they were able to conquer the French. They did this by drawing the French into the open by using a false retreat technique similar to that employed against them by the Normans 300 years earlier, and killing the French by the thousands.

1414 A.D.

The Battle of Agincourt was the last big battle won by English archers. The English were outnumbered by the French four to one, but King

Henry V was able to conquer the French mainly by the superior archery ability of the English. Shakespeare wrote of the casualties at this battle in *King Henry V* and indicated that 29 English were slain as opposed to 10,000 French.

1453 A.D.

This marked the end of the Hundred Years' War. The fact that the English archers were superior to the French is historically significant both to these countries and to America as we know it. What if the French had won? The sixteenth century was marked by religious and social upheaval in England and the subsequent exploratory migrations to America. It is doubtful if the latter would have occurred if the French had won the Hundred Years' War. America would have been settled, but the political, social and religious structures could have been entirely different. The edict by Edward III requiring all Englishmen to practice archery did shape history, especially American history!

1455-1471 A.D.

The Wars of the Roses came about due to the feudal power of some English lords who gained their strength during the preceding century. These men hired professional military archers who were returning from France. Generally, the soldiers did a poor job because they lacked military leadership and discipline. The last battle during the Wars of the Roses was at Tewkesbury. The bow and arrow was still a prominent weapon at that time, but firearms were used also.

1545 A.D.

Roger Ascham published his book, *The Schole of Shootynge*, the first book ever written in the English language which discussed archery tackle and archery techniques. This classic textbook was also published under the title of *Toxophilus.*

1588 A.D.

The English and Spanish used firearms rather extensively at the invasion of the Spanish Armada. Most toxophilites use this battle to denote the decline of archery as a weapon of war but archers were used on a smaller scale in battles for the next 200 years.

1917-1965 A.D.

During World War I, World War II and the Korean War, the bow and arrows were used as a weapon of war. This seems preposterous in the atomic age, but it is true. Some military missions call for killing people very quietly. There are not too many ways to do this, especially from a distance. Expert archers are trained for sniper duties, reconnaissance work and sabotage by the military. Special arrows are made for demolition work, killing by hemorrhage and by impact. Marines train men for this type of activity in their reconnaissance companies, and the army trains special Ranger groups in the ancient arts of killing human beings silently. An arrow at short range has greater penetrating power potential than a .45 calibre bullet and an archer has a better chance of surviving such a mission than a man who kills with a noisy pistol.

Archery in Literature and Art

The bow and arrow have been a part of man's tools since the upper paleolithic period; consequently, it is not surprising to find references made to archery feats in literature and art of mankind. This chapter is concerned with selected references to literary works and works of art where the authors or artists have referred to archery feats or archers in their works. The student of archery is encouraged to look for other literature and art where archery is involved.

LITERATURE

There is considerable mythology surrounding the constellation Sagittarius. Sagittarius is a large southern constellation which the Greeks called a centaur. The centaur was supposed to be shooting an arrow. The term "sagittarius" actually means *the archer.* Sagittarius is located south of Aquila and it is partly in the Milky Way. It is east of Antares, one of the central stars in the constellation known as Scorpio. Sagittarius can be seen during the months of August and September in the United States. Figure 23 shows a schematic diagram of Sagittarius.

The various stars within Sagittarius form parts of the archer and his bow and arrow. Rukbat is the archer's knee; Arkab is the archer's tendon; Ascella is the archer's armpit; Media is the mid-point of the bow and Al Nasl is the arrow point. As the reader will note, it took a vivid imagination to visualize an archer amidst that cellestial configuration.

Greek mythological literature called the centaur of Sagittarius Chiron. Chiron was the famous son of Philyra and Saturn who changed himself into a horse to escape from his wife. Ovid noted that Chiron was slain by Hercules with a poisoned arrow. Jupiter, the Father of the Gods, was responsible for placing Chiron among the constellations according to the myth. Ovid wrote: "Midst Golden Stars he stands refulgent now and thrusts

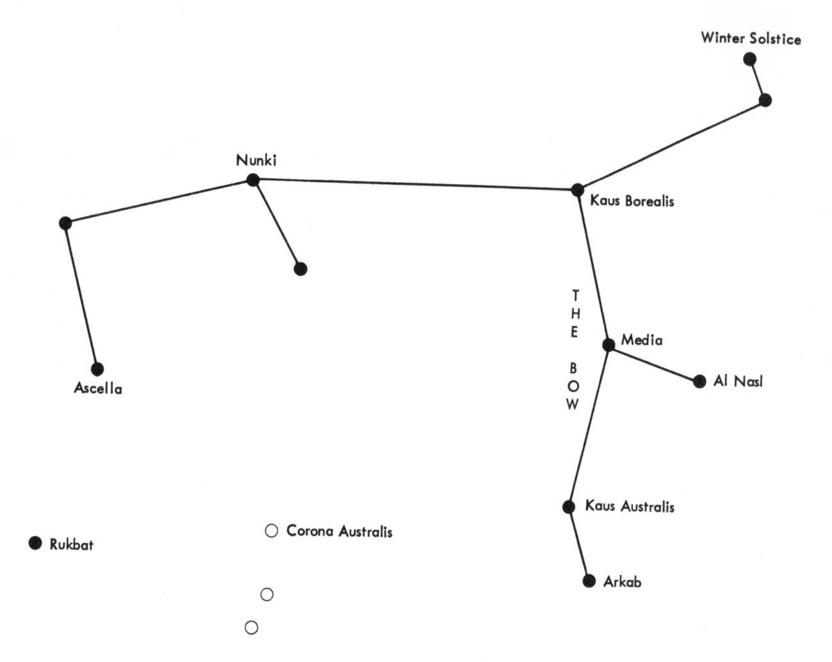

Figure 23—Sagittarius

the Scorpion with his bended bow." The reference is to the relationship between Al Nasl and Antares.

Apollo was the God of Archery. He was credited with numerous extraordinary feats with the bow and arrow. One of the most famous of these mythological events was supposed to take place on Mount Parnassus. A great python was raiding the families who lived in the area. The python smashed homes and ate human beings as if it were going out of style. Apollo decided to put an end to all of that, so he took his bow and arrows in pursuit of the python. He found the python and invited him to fight. As is the case in most myths, good triumphed over evil. Apollo fought the python for four hours and finally killed him with an accurately placed arrow. Shortly following the battle with the python, Apollo encountered Eros or Cupid. He told Eros that a boy should not be playing with a man's weapons. The reference was to the bow and arrow. This, of course, enraged Eros. Eros decided to get even with Apollo, and he did this by shooting him with a golden arrow of love. This arrow caused Apollo to fall in love with Daphne. Daphne was the daughter of Peneun, the river god. Eros

Can you name the five muscle groups which keep the archer upright?

Evaluation Questions
ANTI-GRAVITY
MUSCLES

promptly shot Daphne with a lead arrow of hate. This caused Daphne to hate Apollo so much that she turned herself into a laurel tree. Apollo, in love with her to the end, showed his undying love for her by hanging his bow and quiver on her limbs.

Eros had many adventures in mythological literature with his bow and arrow. The term "eros" is rather interesting. It serves as the root word for the term "erotic," which coincides with the purpose of the existence of Eros. The term "eros" also gave rise to the term "arrows."

One of the greatest mythological archers was Hercules or Herakles. Hercules is better known for his feats of strength, but he was also responsible for many remarkable accomplishments with the bow and arrow. For example, he was primarily responsible for the conquest of Troy due to his prowess with the bow and arrow. Hercules killed Paris with one of his arrows during the Trojan War. Earlier, it will be remembered that Paris had shot Achilles with a poisoned arrow. That was described as a remarkable archery shot, because Achilles' heel area was the only vulnerable area on his body. Anatomists later called the tendon from the gastrocnemius and soleus muscles to the heel "the Achilles Tendon."

There is another minor constellation known as Sagitta, The Arrow. This constellation is located in the Milky Way just north of the constellation called The Eagle. In comparing and discussing Sagittarius and Sagitta, Aratos wrote, "There's further shot another Arrow but this with a bow. Towards it The Bird more northward flies." The references are to Sagittarius and The Eagle. Eratosthenes considered Sagitta to be the shaft with which Apollo exterminated the Cyclops. It was also referred to as one of Cupid's arrows in mythological literature.

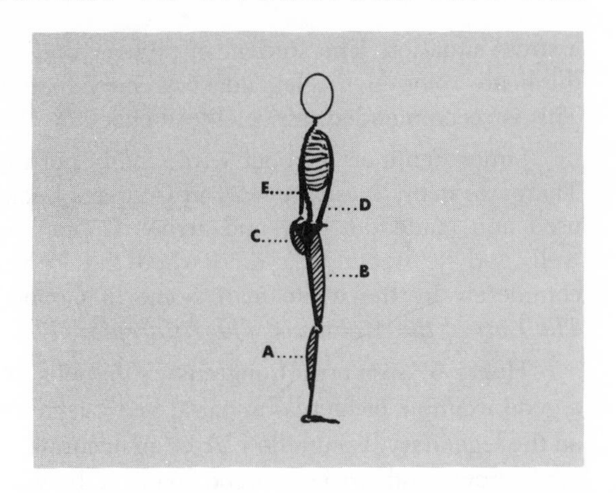

Diagram F:
ANTI-GRAVITY MUSCLES

As we move forward historically, we find other mythological characters. Robin Hood fits into this category. There is no strong evidence to support the fact that such a person actually lived. It is possible, however. As his legend grew, the truth about his feats with the bow and arrow could have been distorted. This is a common characteristic of mythology, i.e., one is apt to find subject matter which can be historically substantiated combined with feats and episodes which are pure myths.

There is a grave in England which is supposed to be occupied by the late Robin Hood. A portion of his epitaph reads, ". . . No archer was like him so good; His wildness named him Robin Hood." (His real name was supposed to be Robert, Earl of Huntington.) It is rather interesting that the vernacular term for someone who lives a rather obstreporous life outside the law is "hood."

Johann Christoph Friedrich von Schiller wrote a play which featured a most dramatic arrow shot. This was *Wilhelm Tell.* The tale centered around the Swiss archer who had the courage and archery skill to defy the invading regime. He was able to demonstrate his skill as an archer by shooting through an apple while it sat on his son's head.

The reader may want to try to duplicate Wilhelm Tell's feat. It is recommended that the apple be hung from a string next to a target instead of being placed on someone's head. Recently, twenty-four beginning archers were given an opportunity to duplicate Tell's shot. They were positioned on the twenty yard line. If someone would have been holding the apple on his head, he would have had 23 arrows in his chest, shoulders, and viscera! One arrow pierced the apple cleanly. A shot like Tell's in real life would have been remarkable, because the father had to shoot at his son in a stress situation. The student of archery and literature may want to try to duplicate some of the legendary archery feats found within the literature. This is recommended, especially to check on their validity.

James Fenimore Cooper wrote many portrayals of the American Indian. There are many factual events in Cooper's books regarding how the Indian used and made the bow and arrow. Cooper researched his material very well, and he wrote at a time when the Indian had not been conquered completely by the white man. Some of Cooper's books are *The Pioneers, The Last of the Mohicans, The Pathfinder, The Deerslayer and The Prairie.*

Henry Wadsworth Longfellow's famous poem, *Song of Hiawatha,* is a good example of factual material being combined with feats which border on the legendary. Longfellow gives an accurate account of how some Indians made bows and arrows. Iagoo made a bow for Hiawatha from ash and the arrows were made of oak. Flint was used for the point, and the bowstring was of dried deer skin. Longfellow also described Hiawatha as being so fast a foot that he could shoot an arrow on a horizontal trajectory and then outrun the arrow. That is fast even with the poor and inefficient tackle of an Indian! If any archery student should duplicate this feat, he should report to the nearest track coach immediately!

Longfellow also mentioned that Hiawatha could shoot ten arrows vertically so fast that the last arrow would be flying skyward before the first arrow had fallen. This is a very difficult feat, and it would be virtually impossible with the tackle described in the poem.

It is recommended that the archery student look for such feats in literature and analyze them regarding their feasibility. If possible, he should try to duplicate them on the archery range. This can be rather interesting at times. Many authors have utilized archery feats in their writing. The reader is referred to the following partial list as a start:

1. Aeschylus. *The Agamemnon.*
2. Arnold, Elliot. *Blood Brother.*
3. Clemens, Samuel. *A Connecticut Yankee in King Arthur's Court.*
4. Defore, Daniel. *The Adventures of Robinson Crusoe.*
5. Gillespy, Frances. *Laymon's Brut: A Comparative Study in Narrative Art.*
6. Homer. *The Illiad and Odyssey.*
7. Lucian. *Dialogues of the Gods.*
8. Millar, George. *A Crossbowman's Story.*
9. Morley, Christopher. *The Arrow.*

10. Ovid. *The Metamorphoses.*
11. Shakespeare, William. *Macbeth.*
12. ————. *Pericles.*
13. Stephenson, Robert Louis. *The Black Arrow.*
14. Swift, Jonathon. *Gulliver's Travels into Several Remote Nations of the World.*
15. Thucydides. *The Peloponnesian War.*

ART

There are thousands of sculps and drawings involving archery in private collections, museums and art museums throughout the world. Some of these, like the Bayeux Tapestry, are very famous and others are obscure. Some of the earliest art forms of mankind, cave drawings, depicted bowhunters in pursuit of game. The student who is interested in art is invited to look for art which involves archery as he pursues his studies.

The works of art* on the following pages show various artists' concepts of archery feats, tackle and events. The reader should study these works and look for the following points: (1) the artist's concept of form, (2) tackle design and (3) the artistic merit of the artist's work.

Diana—Goddess of Wild Things

Cupid With Bow—Chas. Lemiore (Louvre)

---

*(Courtesy of H. Armstrong Roberts. Printed by permission.)

Sennacherib (Assyria)

Roman War Elephant

Battle of Marathon—Briggs: Beale

Richard Pardons Robin Hood—
1184 A.D.—Briggs: Beale

Buffalo Hunt With Wolfskin Mask—Catlin #13

Potential Values to the Archer

The values of muscular activity can be many. Each sport makes unique contributions to its spectators and participants. To derive potential biophysical values an individual must act in an overt fashion. Some values may be derived covertly, but the spectator can never realize the full spectrum of values which a sport offers. One must become involved. The *participant,* unskilled or skilled, is the individual who derives the most benefit of sport from axiological, psychological, physiological and anatomical points of view.

Archery is usually thought of as an "easy sport" by those not cognizant of its many aspects. Granted, target practice in one's backyard or on the local archery range may not be as vigorous as a game of handball or tennis, but in contrast these are not as vigorous as bow hunting for grizzly bear in the high, wilderness areas of Canada or Alaska. *Archery is a sport which the participant can adjust to his own needs and physiological status.* In its many forms it can be engaged in by old and young, men and women, physically handicapped people and superbly conditioned athletes. Archery can be easy, but it can also be extremely difficult in many different ways. Therein lie many potential values of considerable magnitude for the archer.

One major criticism of our society made by sociologists and psychologists is the decline of family unity. To paraphrase a familiar theological statement: the family that plays together stays together. With the onset during the past decade of a wide variety of avocational activities for children and adult-centered activities for children, the family in modern America often finds itself literally going in different directions during its leisure time. Archery is one sport which can be enjoyed by all members of the family at one time at home, on a field archery range, bow hunting, bow fishing or on a target archery range. There are psychological and sociological values inherent within an activity such as archery which make for family unity. This makes archery somewhat unique among sports.

Contrary to popular belief, there is no evidence to support the concept that archery automatically contributes to the development of good posture. Archery does have this potential *if* it is *practiced* extensively *by young children* and *young adults* who have not reached anatomical and physiological maturation.

Can archery be of value to the adult who has round shoulders? It can be of some benefit by lengthening muscles which are abnormally shortened. People who work at desks have a natural tendency to let their scapulae abduct. This lengthens muscles in the back and shortens muscles in the chest. Holding this position for prolonged periods causes physical discomfort. Furthermore, breathing can be inhibited, and this adds to the tired feeling one has at the end of his working day. Shooting a bow for an hour daily does somewhat counteract the atypical muscular actions caused by prolonged sitting. To draw a bow, the shoulders must be pulled back as the scapulae are being adducted (Figure 24). Muscles which were lengthened for long periods during the day are shortened by overcoming the resistance of the bow weight. In effect the archer is doing a highly specific type of weight training. The greatest potential benefit from this kind of activity is the ultimate relaxation of muscles used atypically for prolonged periods during the working day.

Figure 24—Scapular Adduction

The archer must utilize a large percentage of his musculature while shooting the bow. The shooting stance requires active functioning of muscles which keep man in an upright position.

The abdominal muscles act in an antigravity fashion if the archer has a slight backward lean as he draws. The large rectus abdominis muscle pulls the archer back into an upright position. For the most part, this type of movement is very subtle. All of these muscles act in a secondary manner to the most important muscle groups required for shooting. The latter are located in the arms, shoulders, shoulder girdle and hands. When an archer shoots in a tournament for a day or hunts for many hours, he must have all of these muscles in condition. More musculature is working when shooting the bow and arrow than meets the eye. Physiologically, this can have considerable value for the archer.

POTENTIAL VALUES TO THE ARCHER

Archery provides the participant with a sport which can be used throughout his life. Some sport activities learned early in life do not have this potential. A man who is in his thirties does not engage in American football during his leisure time even if he was outstanding as a performer in college. In contrast, many excellent archers do not reach their performance peaks until they are well past the age of thirty. "Old people" can enjoy archery just as well as people who are under thirty years of age.

One major biophysical value of muscular activity is the resultant ability to release emotional tension. Emotional tension seems to be cumulative in nature. The reader has probably experienced at least one day in his life when "everything seemed to go wrong!" At the conclusion of such a day, he is rather tired and tense. The tension tends to be psychological. Psychiatrists tell us that it is a good idea to "blow off steam" on these occasions in a socially acceptable way. This has value to one's mental health. Shooting the bow and arrow for an hour in the evening after a "bad day" tends to relax the archer.

The challenges which archery presents in its various sporting forms have value for many people. Archery is not an easy sport to master for there are many opportunities for human errors to occur. This facet of archery has the greatest appeal to the real sportsman and the individual who seeks perfection in the things he attempts in life. *Mastery of archery* could be the motivating factor. There are many people who would take great pride in the fact that they were able to shoot a perfect end from 100 yards in the York Round. This feat would be highly significant to the individual who pursues excellence as a way of life. Things which are difficult to attain can be given value, and perfection in archery is difficult to attain.

The serious student of the humanities may derive some enjoyment by reading and studying about the use of archery as portrayed by many famous authors and scholars throughout history. The mythological literature abounds with stories about archery, and art museums throughout the world contain many famous works of art which depict archers in action. The scholarly student who is interested in archery should look for these literary and artistic works as he pursues his formal education.

The individual who enjoys social activities will find that archery is a good medium for him. Most cities of any size in the United States have archery clubs which provide places for the archer to share his interest with fellow archers. The clubs are locally operated by a system of self-government and dues which average approximately $30.00 per year. Rounds are shot periodically for practice. There are intraclub and interclub tournaments. Members also compete in large professional and amateur national tournaments. Membership in such a club offers the archer fellowship with people who have similar avocational interests. This has value for many people.

In contrast to the social aspect of archery, the archer who likes to be alone can practice and compete on an individual basis. No partner or team is absolutely necessary. The archer may enjoy any phase of archery by himself if he desires. It has been said that the greatest form of competition is with one's self. An archer can compete with or without direct contact with other people.

As has been shown, archery is and has been many things to many people. In our contemporary society it is a sport for a real competitor. It is for the individual who enjoys handling fine tackle; it is for the man or woman who enjoys being in the out-of-doors during a hunting session, a field archery tournament or bow fishing; it is for the person who enjoys the spirit of competition with other people and with himself. Archery can be a partial means of making the participant's leisure time more rewarding and meaningful.

SELECTED BIBLIOGRAPHY

Archery Magazine. National Field Archery Association, Box H, Palm Springs, California 92262.

Ascham, Roger. *Toxophilus*. London: A. Murray and Son, 1545.

Bow and Arrow Magazine. 550-A South Citrus Avenue, Covina, California.

Burke, Edmund. *The History of Archery*. New York: William Morrow and Company, 1957.

Davis, Elwood Craig, Gene A. Logan and Wayne C. McKinney. *Biophysical Values of Muscular Activity* (second edition). Dubuque: Wm. C. Brown Publishing Company, 1965.

Elmer, Robert P. and Nabih A. Faris. *Arab Archery*. New Jersey: Princeton University Press, 1945.

Elmer, Robert P. *Archery*. Philadelphia: The Penn Publishing Company, 1926.

Herrigel, Eugen. *Zen in the Art of Archery*. New York: Pantheon Books, 1953.

Hickman, C. N., F. Nagler and Paul E. Klopsteg. *Archery: The Technical Side*. Redlands, California: Box 388, N.F.A.A., 1947.

Hill, Howard. *Hunting the Hard Way*. Chicago: Follett Publishing Company, 1953.

Hougham, Paul C. *The Encyclopedia of Archery.* New York: A. S. Barnes and Company, 1957.

Klopsteg, P. E. "Physics of Bows and Arrows," *American Journal of Physics,* 11:175-92, August, 1943.

Love, Albert J. *Field Archery Technique.* Corpus Christi: Dotson Printing Company, 1956.

McKinney, Wayne C. "The Effect of Correlated Academic Subject Matter on the Acquisition of a Motor Skill," unpublished research, University of Southern California, 1962.

National Field Archery Association. *Official Handbook of Field Archery.* Route 2, Box 514, Redlands, California.

Pope, Saxton. *Yahi Archery.* Berkeley: University of California Press, 1918.

Pope, Saxton. *Hunting With Bow and Arrow.* New York: G. P. Putnam's Sons, 1947.

Pope, Saxton. *The Adventurous Bowmen.* New York: G. P. Putnam's Sons, 1926.

Rhode, Robert J. *Archery Champions.* Norristown: The Archer's Publishing Company, 1961.

Tam and Archery World. National Archery Association. 7 South Chestnut Street, Boyertown, Pennsylvania, 1951.

Thompson, Maurice. *The Witchery of Archery.* New York: Charles Scribner's Sons, 1878.

Wilson, R. I. (Ed.) *Basic Instruction for Classes.* Hickory Corners, Michigan: Professional Archers Association, 1964.

ARCHERY

WM. C. BROWN COMPANY PUBLIS

DUBUQUE